THE ROLE OF A LIFETIME

THE SCRIPT GOD WROTE FOR WOMEN

Claudia Barba

journeyforth®

Greenville, South Carolina

Cover photo: iStockphoto.com © zbruch (curtain)

The Role of a Lifetime—The Script God Wrote for Women
Claudia Barba

Design by Nathan Hutcheon
Page layout by Michael Boone

Greenville, South Carolina 29614
JourneyForth Books is a division of BJU Press.

Printed in the United States of America

ISBN 978-1-62856-022-0

15 14 13 12 11 10 9 8 7 6 5 4 3 2 1

For my mother
Elizabeth Horne Holmes
(1921–2010)

My model for life and ministry
and my friend

Contents

Prologue

What joy it is to be a woman! We were made in God's image and given unique abilities for the extraordinary role He has written for us. God has a marvelous plan for every woman who will give her life to Him and live His way.

Women do face tough challenges. That's the fault of Satan, who spread his own rebellion to earth and so brought painful consequences into the life of every woman since Eve. That sad story makes up *Act One* of our study.

In the fullness of time our Messiah, Jesus Christ, made His entrance onto earth's stage to redeem us from the curse of sin. While He was here, He proved Himself the special friend and protector of women, even dying on the cross to be our Savior. That's *Act Two.*

Now Christ continues to work out His purposes for us through His church, where both men and women can serve Him by serving others. And that's *Act Three.*

No woman is a minor player in God's drama of the ages. If you will stick with His script and follow His directions, He will perfect His plan for you, using you and blessing you far beyond anything you could ever imagine. Being a woman of God is the role of a lifetime—a role written just for you.

ACT 1

Woman in the Garden

CHAPTER ONE

Created in His Image

GENESIS 1:26–27

And God said, Let us make man in our image, after our likeness: . . . So God created man in his own image, in the image of God created he him; male and female created he them.

Created in the image of God—what a privilege! But what does it mean? He's God and we're not, so how can we possibly be like Him? And we're born as male or female. Which gender is God? Both? Neither? Does it matter? The answers to these questions are in the Bible, the book He "breathed out" so we could know the truth about Him and about ourselves.

Thy word is truth. (John 17:17)

Until you know who God is, you cannot understand yourself, for you are made in His image. So let's begin with some basics about God.

God Is a Person

A person has intellect.

God knows.

He that planted the ear, shall he not hear? he that formed the eye, shall he not see? He that chastiseth the heathen,

> shall not he correct? he that teacheth man knowledge, shall not he know? (Psalm 94:9–10)

God not only knows everything; He is the source of all knowledge.

A person can feel.

Women know all about emotions! God has feelings too, and He expresses them, never as an impulsive or unrestrained response to upsetting or bewildering circumstances, but by His own deliberate choice.

1. What are some of His emotions?

   John 3:16

   love
   ___

   Genesis 6:6

   grief
   ___

   Psalm 7:11

   anger
   ___

   Zephaniah 3:17

   Happiness
   ___

   Isaiah 53:3

   Sorrow
   ___

A person has a will.

God makes choices and plans. (See Rom. 8:28; Eph. 1:4–5; 2:10.) Nobody can frustrate His sovereign will: "For the Lord of hosts hath purposed, and who shall disannul [frustrate] it? and his hand is stretched out, and who shall turn it back?" (Isa. 14:27).

A person has relationships.

2. Who were two of God's special friends?

   James 2:23

   Abraham

   Exodus 33:11

   Moses

   According to John 15:13–15, who else does He call His friends?

   those who obey God

To Think and Talk About

How could you respond scripturally to someone who says, "God is not a person but simply an energy force in the universe. *God* is a word like *gravity* or *love*—a name we have invented for invisible influences or powers we don't understand or can't explain."?

We were created in His image, had feelings, had a will, and had friends (relationships).

God is spirit.

In John 4, Jesus sat by a well talking to a Samaritan woman who believed that God could be worshiped in only one place. While explaining the error in her thinking, He said, "God is a Spirit," or more literally, "God is spirit (*pneuma)*" (4:24). Paul the Apostle later described God as someone who is:

Eternal: He was never born and will never die. (See 1Tim. 1:17.) Forever and ever

Immortal: He is incorruptible and cannot decay. (See Rom. 1:23.)

Invisible: He cannot be seen. (See Col. 1:15.)

Jesus Christ was for a time "made in the likeness of men" (Phil. 2:7), "made flesh" (John 1:14), and lived on earth as a male human so He could die as a blood sacrifice for our sin. The triune God, however, is always described in Scripture as Spirit, not flesh. As Spirit, He is free from all bodily limitations and definitions, including any characteristics of gender.

But in order for us to comprehend one who otherwise would be way beyond our understanding, God presents Himself as having characteristics familiar to us. To help our finite minds grasp the nature of an infinite God, the inspired writers of Scripture sometimes used a literary device called *anthropomorphism*—attributing human traits to the non-human.

3. Find the anthropomorphisms in 1 Peter 3:12. What do they help you to understand about God and how He relates to His creatures?

   He watches over us and is waiting to hear from us always.

God has revealed himself to us.

As female?

To help us appreciate His sacrificial love and devotion to His children, God sometimes describes Himself as having qualities that we usually think of as motherly.

4. What traits of God are revealed in Isaiah 49:15?

   always thinking and having compassion for us.

   And in Isaiah 66:13?

   He wants to comfort us.

   What did Jesus compare Himself to in Matthew 23:37?

   Hen protecting her chicks.

What honor God gives mothers when He compares His love to ours. But God is no more a mother than Jesus Christ was a mother hen! Word pictures like these simply help us to understand who God is to us.

As male?

From to the beginning to the end of His Word, God presents Himself to us as male.

5. Circle the masculine pronouns in the following verses. There are a lot of them.

   And on the seventh day God ended his work which he had made; and he rested on the seventh day from all his work which he had made. (Genesis 2:2)

   Only fear the Lord, and serve him in truth with all your heart: for consider how great things he hath done for you. (1 Samuel 12:24)

   He maketh me to lie down in green pastures: he leadeth me beside the still waters. He restoreth my soul: he leadeth me in the paths of righteousness for his name's sake. (Psalm 23:2–3)

   Behold, the Lord God will come with strong hand, and his arm shall rule for him: behold, his reward is with him, and his work before him. (Isaiah 40:10)

   The Lord is good, a strong hold in the day of trouble; and he knoweth them that trust in him. (Nahum 1:7)

   For God so loved the world, that he gave his only begotten Son, that whosoever believeth in him should not perish, but have everlasting life. (John 3:16)

   God is no respecter of persons: But in every nation he that feareth him, and worketh righteousness, is accepted with him. (Acts 10:34–35)

> But God, who is rich in mercy, for his great love wherewith he loved us. (Ephesians 2:4)

> Fear God, and give glory to him; for the hour of his judgment is come: and worship him that made heaven, and earth, and the sea, and the fountains of waters. (Revelation 14:7)

This is just a sampling of the myriad of masculine pronouns used to refer to God in every accurate translation of the Bible. He never—not even once—inspired the writers of Scripture to refer to any member of the Trinity as *she*. Almost 1200 times in the New Testament, the name for God is *theos,* a masculine noun in Greek. There are approximately 170 references in the Bible to God as *father*, and not a single one as *mother*. Here are a few of them.

> Wherefore David blessed the Lord before all the congregation: and David said, Blessed be thou, Lord God of Israel our **father**, forever and ever. (1 Chronicles 29:10)

> But now, O Lord, thou art our **father**; we are the clay, and thou our potter; and we all are the work of thy hand. (Isaiah 64:8)

> After this manner therefore pray ye: Our **Father** which art in heaven, Hallowed be thy name. (Matthew 6:9)

> For ye have not received the spirit of bondage again to fear; but ye have received the Spirit of adoption, whereby we cry, Abba, **Father**. (Romans 8:15)

Read John 14:1–13 and notice how often Jesus spoke of God as His Father. The evidence is overwhelming: God wants us to know Him as a *he*. But there is a current theological movement to create a new image of God by referring to the Divine One as *she*. By this point, you should be able to see that anyone who does that is showing either ignorance or deliberate denial of what the Bible teaches. Does it matter? Yes! It's idolatry to create and worship a god you prefer, a god you have created with your hands or in your mind and imagination, rather than the one true God as revealed in the Bible.

> Thou shalt have no other gods before me. (Exodus 20:3)

> Ye shall not go after other gods, of the gods of the people which are round about you. (Deuteronomy 6:14)

To Think and Talk About

> How would you respond to someone who suggests you pray to God as *she*?

Ask them to show you one reference in the Bible where God is referred to a she. Show them all kinds of references of God as "He" or "Father."

God created us in His image.

> So God created man in his own image, in the image of God created he him; male and female created he them. (Genesis 1:27)

> Male and female created he them; and blessed them, and called their name Adam [human being], in the day when they were created. (Genesis 5:2)

We are not exact replicas of God. We can't do what He can do. We're not all-powerful, all-knowing, or present everywhere at once. Though our souls will live somewhere forever, our bodies will eventually die. And we cannot look like God, for He has no physical form. Being made in His image simply means that both men and women are persons in the same way that God is a person.

We have intellect. We know. We learn. We are imaginative and creative.

We have feelings. We express a variety of passions and emotions.

We have wills. We make decisions.

We have relationships. We have friendships with other people, and we interact with God.

When you laugh or cry with a friend, write a love note, compose a tune, play with your child, balance your checkbook, cook a meal, paint a picture, pray, memorize a Bible verse, obey the speed limit, or ask for forgiveness, you are showing that you are not a highly-evolved animal, but a person made in His image. As a living soul, you have enormous potential to glorify your Creator through accurate knowledge of truth, virtuous creativity, godly choices, disciplined emotions, and edifying relationships. Your life can give Him glory.

To Think and Talk About

Scientists and sociologists sometimes use their study of social and sexual activity in the animal kingdom to determine acceptable behavior for *human animals*. What do you think about that?

6. In what ways does the Bible say all humans—male or female—are alike? Look for the *all* and *whosoever* words in these verses.

   Romans 3:23

   all have sinned

   Romans 10:9–13

   all can be saved - if they believe

   John 3:16

   if they believe, they can have eternal life

   Galatians 3:26–28

   can be heirs of Christ

   2 Corinthians 5:10

   all be ~~judged~~ judged

Jew and Gentile, slave and free, male and female—we are all sinners called to repent of our sin and trust Jesus as Savior. At the foot of the cross, there is perfect gender equality, for there the blessings of salvation are lavished on men and women alike. His love is equally ours, and so are our privileges, for we are "one in Christ Jesus" (Gal. 3:28), united in His body, the church. Someday we will live together in heaven without distinctions. Only the Lord could unite men and women like that, because we are very different creatures. Those differences are part of His excellent plan, and they are for our good, as we'll learn in our next lesson.

CHAPTER TWO

Created with Differences

Made in His image; persons with minds, emotions, wills, and relationships; equal in standing before God—in these ways men and women are alike. But we are also very different! The physical distinctions between us did not evolve over eons, nor did the differences in gender roles develop just as an expedient way to organize society. They are part of God's original creative plan, and they are for our good.

Once again, let's start with something basic: how many genders are there? The answer may seem absurdly obvious. But it actually isn't, not in a world that's being increasingly influenced by the belief that gender is a spectrum with a wide range of categories besides just male and female, or the viewpoint that gender identity is a product of parental training and social experiences regardless of the sexual characteristics present at birth. Some are promoting the right of any person at any age to select, declare, and enjoy the public and private privileges of a preferred gender—male, female, or something (invented) in between.

Belief in gender as a spectrum is being taught in schools and argued in courtrooms. It is being written into law and becoming part of public policy. But the Bible leaves no room for doubt: in God's blueprint there is no *gender spectrum* with unlimited variations of male/female identities. There are two genders—only two. Sexual distinctions were instituted for all humanity in the Garden of Eden, and God determines each individual's gender at conception. Any effort to blur or erase gender distinctions in society as a whole or to alter one's own God-given gender, defies and insults the Creator.

> In the image of God created he him; male and female created he them. (Genesis 1:27)

Jesus Christ, who was God incarnate, validated the truth of only two genders by quoting this verse as He taught about marriage in Matthew 19:4 and Mark 10:6. Every human being is either male or female. This was true in the Garden of Eden, true when Jesus was on earth, and is still true today. Truth does not change with the years or with shifting public policy.

> Christ will never accommodate his morality to the times, nor to the inclinations of men. What was done at the beginning is what God judged most worthy of his glory, most profitable for man, and most suitable to nature.[1]

God Created Two Genders

> For in six days the Lord made heaven and earth, the sea, and all that in them is. (Exodus 20:11)

After creating light and dividing it from the darkness, God made the sky and separated it from the waters below. Then He divided the seas from the dry land and added the sun, moon, and stars to the sky to mark the divisions between days and nights, seasons and years. Next He placed sea creatures in the oceans and parted them from the birds in the sky. Do you notice all the separations? On the sixth day there was one more separation when God made His masterpiece—humans—and divided them into two distinct genders.

The male human was made first.

> And the Lord God formed man of the dust of the ground, and breathed into his nostrils the breath of life; and man became a living soul. (Genesis 2:7)

Adam was made from dust. But he was worth much more than his weight in dirt, for immediately God did for Adam something that He had not done for any other creature.

1. What did God do?

   ~~became~~ breathed life in man & he became a living soul.

   And that changed everything. With the breath of God, what did Adam become?

   a living soul.

   This man was unique in all creation. What were Adam's first two tasks? (See Gen. 2:15, 19–20.)

   Keep the garden and name all the animals

   All the beasts and birds came to Adam to be given their names. Who was missing?

   a helper for Adam

It's likely that the creatures paraded before Adam in male and female pairs. When the parade ended, Adam still stood alone, for not one of those creatures was like him. None was made in God's image, none his counterpart, none suitable to be his helper and companion. No creature but Adam was a living soul. At the end of each day of creation, God had consistently pronounced His creative work good. (See Gen. 1:4, 10, 12, 18, 21, 25.)

2. But what did He say about Adam's aloneness? (See Gen. 2:18.)

   not good for him.

What did He decide to do about it?

make him a helper

God Created Two Genders with Differences

To create another human, God could have cloned Adam, but instead He chose to make an entirely new creature with a unique design and purpose and of a different gender. It wasn't until the early twentieth century that genetic researchers began to decode God's gender-determination plan—XX chromosomes appear only in females; XY chromosomes are the marker of maleness. The gender distinctions (dress, hairstyles, division of labor) that have appeared in some form in every culture in every era are the practical outworking of the truth that He made us to be different—different from the very beginning, different at our cores.

To Think and Talk About

Is it possible to alter one's gender by changing clothing, hairstyle, makeup, or mannerisms? Or through plastic surgery and hormone treatments? At what biological level would gender reassignment have to take place?

3. The new creature was made from a *different substance.* What was it? (See Gen. 2:21–22.)

one of Adam's ribs

In some versions of Scripture, the word *rib* is translated as *side.* But whether God used just one rib or more of the bones and tissues from Adam's side, Adam recognized that Eve had been formed from his flesh and bone, and that joined together they would become *one flesh* in the union we call marriage. She was like him, created in God's image; but she was also different, designed to complement him in every way.

How alluring the first woman must have been to the first man! In her honor, Adam (obviously not a grunting caveman but an intelligent being with complex language skills) composed the world's first love poem. You can read it in Genesis 2:23. In this short stanza, he gave her a *different name* from his.

> She was to be called "_Woman_, because she was _taken_ _out_ of Man."

(In the same way that men and women are related as humans but different as persons, words for the two genders are often related with the same root form but different in meaning. For example, in Hebrew they are *ish/ishshah,* and in English *male/female* and *man/woman.* You may be able to think of examples from other languages.)

4. The new human was also given a *different role*. What was it? (See Gen. 2:18.)

   help Adam

   ____

"Help meet" is the English translation of two Hebrew words. One is *'ezer,* which simply means *help.* Joined together, those two Hebrew words in various translations describe Eve's role as:

> "one like himself as a help to him" (BBE)
>
> "a helper suitable for him" (NASB)
>
> "a helper comparable to him" (NKJV)
>
> "a helper fit for him" (ESV)
>
> "his counterpart" (LEB)

Every other time it is used in the Scriptures, the word 'ezer refers to God as our helper.

> Our soul waiteth for the Lord: he is our help ['ezer] and our shield. (Psalm 33:20)

> I will lift up mine eyes unto the hills, from whence cometh my help ['ezer]. My help ['ezer] cometh from the Lord, which made heaven and earth. (Psalm 121:1–2)

To be called *helper* is an honor, for we share this title with God. Of course, the Lord is capable of giving aid way beyond anything that we can do, but still, what a privilege it is to be an 'ezer! [See "Uses of 'ezer" on page 123 in the appendix.]

> What a strong word *helper* is! Think of a partner, a coworker, a supporter, an advocate. This is what we are called to be for our husbands. A helper gives aid and support from a position of strength. . . . God made us "suitable"—fitting, entirely appropriate—for our husbands. What a privilege God has given us.[2]

1 Corinthians 11:8–9 expresses the woman's role like this: "For the man is not of [made from] the woman; but the woman of the man. Neither was the man created for [the sake of] the woman; but the woman for the man." Adam needed an aide, a partner, a colleague, and Eve was made to fill that need.

> The account of the creation of the woman leaves before us a straightforward fact: the woman was created to bring God glory by helping and assisting the man. This is the reason she was made, the earthly definition of her existence. You can accept it or reject it, but the text is clear. The male-female combination, this powerful and perfect, united couple, has a job to do . . . a job neither could do alone.[3]

To Think and Talk About

> How will a woman's daily life and decisions be shaped by her commitment to fill the role of an 'ezer?

Men acknowledge that their work becomes easier when women are their helpers, for women have abilities that men do not have, aptitudes innate to females, skills that complement the strengths and balance the weaknesses of males—and vice versa, of course. Mature, godly women are invaluable helpers to Christian men, whether they are joined to them in marriage or working with them as a team in any other setting. We are crucial, indispensable helpers in our homes, churches, and communities.

And we make life sweeter! When a church my husband pastored in Tennessee was building a new building, I sometimes went to the county office building to pick up permits or deliver documents. It was mostly a dull, gray place with harsh lighting and dreary furnishings—with one exception. One office was a delight to visit, with its colorful rugs and drapes, fresh flowers, and cozy, comfortable seating areas lit by soft lamps. I looked forward to going there and wasn't at all surprised to discover that the person in charge of that department was a woman. Are you?

To Think and Talk About

> Women find it easy to spot men whose clothing, posture, speech, and mannerisms are feminine. How do you respond when you see this? What characteristics are distinctively masculine? How do you think a man reacts when he sees those in a woman? What can you do to avoid showing masculine qualities or appearance? What can you do to honor and maintain the gender differences God established at Creation?

God Created Two Genders for Our Good

Sometimes it seems that men and women are not only from different planets, but from different universes! And yet God planned it this way—and not just to complicate our lives. Marriage is not the joining of two equals, but rather of two opposites with distinctions that make the one-flesh union strong and resilient and help it prosper and endure.

5. Why do you think God made us physically different?

to compliment each other so you work as a team

Why is it good that we don't think alike?

to round each other out. To make us Stronger in areas where we are weaker.

What about our different ways of communicating? Why would God plan it that way?

So we learn how to live with other people - Children, work, church, and in public

Men and women don't express emotions in the same way. How does that work for our good?

makes men more considerate and make women not dwell on things.

To Think and Talk About

Sometimes women are frustrated by male/female differences, even to the point of demeaning men because they aren't like us. Based on what we have just studied from Scripture, how should we respond to those differences? What would a one-gender world be like? Be thankful!

I was replying to a phone survey asking me to rank the customer service at a fast food restaurant. It was one of those "rate your overall satisfaction with the quality of the food served from 1 to 10, with 1 being extremely dissatisfied and 10 being extremely satisfied" sort of surveys. The list of questions was long and tedious, but the promise of a coupon for a free chicken sandwich at the end kept me going. The very last query caught my attention.

"Are you male or female? Press 1 for female and 2 for male." Not "rank your gender on a spectrum of 1 to 10 with 1 being completely female and 10 completely male." Two options. That was all that was needed for we all know instinctively that there are only two genders. The differences between them are buried deeply in our DNA. They are for our good, and when we recognize and preserve them, we bring glory to our Creator.

CHAPTER THREE

Meeting the Enemy

Eve lived in paradise. Everything she could ever want had been provided, including a perfect mate. She and Adam were the only two humans in the world, and they were both sinless and completely compatible. They had fulfilling work to do, an unspoiled natural world to enjoy, and God Himself as a friend to walk with them in the cool of the day. Life in the Garden of Eden was ideal. If any woman should have been content, it was Eve.

But soon she and Adam made a terrible choice and, as a result, were banished from their paradise. After they left, life became hard. For Adam, working the ground turned into drudgery. For Eve, the bright joys of motherhood became tarnished by painful childbirth and by such extreme sibling rivalry that her firstborn son murdered his younger brother.

The perfection of the garden didn't last long, and things have gone downhill ever since. The harmony God designed for marriage is now marred by battles of self-will . . . and worse. How could this happen? How did we get from Eden to here? The answers are in Genesis 3, which tells the saddest story in human history. As you study this chapter, you'll discover that the struggles you face now began long ago with Eve.

Eve's Environment

Her Home

Genesis 2:8–10 gives us some details about the wonders of Eden, Eve's magnificent garden home.

1. Which two special trees are named?

   tree of life

   tree of knowledge of good and evil

   What did Adam and Eve *not* have? (See Gen. 2:25.)

   Clothes

Her Marriage

There's much current political discussion about redefining marriage. But the one who established marriage gave us His unchanging definition of marriage in Genesis 2:24: "Therefore shall a man leave his father and his mother, and shall cleave unto his wife: and they shall be one flesh." Since marriage was God's idea, He gets to make the rules. The only valid definition of marriage is the one written by its Author.

Cleave is one of those odd English words with two opposite meanings. It can mean either *to divide* or *to be joined together.* Here it means *to adhere, to be glued or stuck together*. At marriage, God says, one man and one woman are joined with supernatural superglue!

2. What do the simple, straightforward words of Genesis 2:24 lead any honest reader to conclude about:

   Same-sex marriage?

   it has to be a man to a wife. Male to female

Polygamy?

a man (one) to his wife (singular)

Adultery (a sexual relationship with anyone other than your spouse)?

Even though homosexual marriages are now legal in our country, they are and always will be sinful perversion in the eyes of God. Nothing is clearer in Scripture than that marriage is between one man and one woman. Jesus Himself confirmed this in Mark 10:6–9, and the rest of the Bible consistently condemns homosexual activity. (See Lev. 18:22 and 20:13; Rom. 1:24–32; 1 Cor. 6:9; and the story of the destruction of Sodom and Gomorrah in Gen. 18–19.)

Since it is a portrait of spiritual union, sexual union is restricted to one husband and one wife. When a married couple become intimate partners, when they *know* each other in the way that "Adam knew Eve his wife" (Gen. 4:1), their physical joining is a picture of their becoming *one flesh* in God's eyes.

Since the garden, God's will has been purity before marriage and monogamy afterwards.

3. What argument does Paul make against adultery in 1 Corinthians 6:15–16?

Adam and Eve enjoyed the perfect union that God planned for all married couples: two genders made one flesh, under God, indivisible. We are reminded of God's will for marriage whenever we hear these classic words at the end of wedding ceremonies just before the smiling couple marches back up the aisle: "That which God has joined together let no man put asunder." Marriage, the joining by God of two people of opposite genders in a permanent, exclusive physical and spiritual oneness, is one of His best gifts.

Adam and Eve had an ideal marriage. Since there was no sin, there was no selfishness; and without selfishness, there is no conflict, only perfect unity. "Only by pride cometh contention" (Pro. 13:10). Eve was living out God's ideal plan in a perfect environment with a faultless husband. But then Satan entered the stage and spoiled the lovely scene.

Eve's Temptation

The Setting

God gave Adam and Eve only one restriction.

4. What was the restriction? (See Gen. 2:16–17.)

could not eat of the tree of the knowledge of good and evil

What was the penalty for breaking that rule?

they would surely die

What power did the fruit of the tree of life have? (See Gen. 3:22.)

to give life - forgiveness

You will see this tree of life someday, since it will again appear in heaven, bearing eternal fruit for believers to enjoy (Rev. 2:7; 22:2). "The tree of knowledge of good and evil" was placed in the garden as a way for God to affirm His right to make demands on His creatures. It also gave them an opportunity to show Him their love through their obedience. This tree was a test.

> Man was not made an automaton [robot] who would live for the glory of God without any choice in the matter. His

inclination was toward God, but since he had the power of contrary choice, he could be confirmed in this inclination only by deliberate choice in the presence of the possibility of choosing the opposite.[1]

The Tempter

5. What was Eve's tempter like? (See Gen. 3:1.)

very crafty, cunning, sneaky

Tempter is an interesting word describing one who is cunning in a bad sense: crafty, sly, wily, sneaky, devious, shifty, scheming, deceitful, underhanded, and conniving. Eve's tempter came in the form of a snake (serpent), but in Revelation 12:9 and 20:2 we find out who he really was.

This wicked one continues to be a master of disguise. If he revealed himself as he truly is, people would run away in horror. Just as many poisonous snakes are graceful and encircled with stunning designs, Satan covers himself in the camouflage of all that is beautiful, appealing, reasonable, and interesting.

Satan himself can be transformed to appear as a beautiful angel.

> And no marvel; for Satan himself is transformed into an angel of light. (2 Corinthians 11:14)

To Think and Talk About

Today, one of Satan's primary tools to spread his lies is the media. Television, movies, and popular music are skilled at presenting sin as delightful rather than destructive. What examples can you think of? How can you protect yourself from the Devil's deceptions?

Satan is a created spirit being who was once an "anointed cherub" living in the presence of God but was cast out of heaven.

6. Why was he cast out? What was his ambition? (See Isa. 14:12–14.)

   for his pride - wanted to be higher than God

Read Ezekiel 28:12–19. This passage primarily refers to a proud, wicked king who reigned over Tyre, but there is evidence that in these verses God is speaking to the evil supernatural being behind the king's throne (just as Jesus rebuked Satan for his influence over Peter in Matthew 16:23.) For example, Ezekiel 28:14 tells us that he was a cherub living in heaven, "the holy mount of God."

7. How did Satan look then? (See Eze. 28:12, 17.)

   perfect and beautiful

   How do he and his servants appear now? (See 2 Cor. 11:13–15.)

   utterly cast down

   How intelligent was he? (See Eze. 28:12.)

   Full of wisdom

   What place on earth did he visit? (See Eze. 28:12.)

   Garden of Eden

   Why was he expelled from heaven? (See Eze. 28:12.)

   pride

Your enemy Satan is clever enough not to show you his authentic, hideous self. He appears captivating and congenial instead, just as he approached Eve as a handsome, charming friend. She did not run from him, though he was occupying the body of a snake. At this point serpents did not yet crawl on their bellies (that came later in Genesis 3:14) but probably stood upright. Maybe Adam and Eve were able to communicate with animals in a way that is unknown to us today or perhaps the serpent had the power of speech. In any case, Satan was in control of this serpent and spoke through him.

Knowing that Eve could be tempted, he came as she stood near the tree of knowledge of good and evil. Follow their conversation in Genesis 3:1–5. When Satan asked, "Has God really said that you cannot eat of every tree in the garden?" it was more than a simple question.

8. What was he insinuating?

that God just didn't want them to be as wise as He.

Doubts

Satan was planting doubts in Eve's mind about something he actually knew was true. Because he once lived in God's presence, he knew that God does not lie. (See Titus 1:2.) Compare Eve's answer to Satan in Genesis 3:2–3 and God's instructions in 2:16–17.

9. What word did Eve omit?

What detail did she add? Why do you think she did that?

can't even touch it

Satan is still working to make women doubt God's words. Steadfast confidence in the Bible is the bedrock that will keep you stable through life's trials and Satan's enticements. Doubts about the Word of God will shift you onto shaky ground where you will wobble during troubles and temptations, and that is exactly where Satan wants you to be.

10. When misgivings about the truth of God's Word pass through your mind, where are they coming from? How can you fight them off?

Satan, Search scripture for truth!

To Think and Talk About

A woman who is desperate for help with a problem may seek help from some sort of personal spirit guide. You probably already know to beware of those who call themselves *mediums* or *psychics* and anyone who claims the power to communicate with unseen spirits. (If you wonder about this, study Leviticus 19:31 and Deuteronomy 18:10–13.) But the idea that we can look to spirit beings other than God for help, protection, guidance, courage, or inspiration has recently become a recurring theme in the media. Where have you heard it? In the light of Eve's story and of 1 John 4:1, how should you respond to this popular but mistaken message?

Denial

Then Satan revealed his true identity: he is a liar and the source of all lies.

> There is no truth in him. When he speaketh a lie, he speaketh of his own: for he is a liar, and the father of it. (John 8:44)

He told Eve two lies: God's words are not true, and God is not good.

In Genesis 3:4, the serpent (empowered by Satan) directly denied God's words when he spoke his first lie: "You shall not surely die."

His second lie is in verse 5. Doing what God had forbidden, he promised, would not hurt Eve but would instead be good for her: "For God doth know that in the day ye eat thereof, then your eyes shall be opened, and ye shall be as gods, knowing good and evil." By putting the fruit off-limits, Satan suggested, God was doing more than just withholding physical pleasure. He was denying Adam and Eve the privilege of being as wise as He is, of knowing all that He knows. God, the Devil implied, doesn't want you to be happy or smart. He is selfish and mean, so He is not good.

To Think and Talk About

> When were you last tempted to think that God's Word might not be true? That He is not good? That He doesn't care about you? That He was denying you something you deserve? What circumstances most often cause women to believe Satan's lies?

Does it seem that we've gotten sidetracked by our study of Satan? Remember this: if you're a woman, Eve's enemy is your enemy too. He attackes your home and family by making adultery look desirable, divorce routine, homosexuality inevitable, and abortion insignificant. And he attacks your mind, emotions, and will. Like an ever-ravenous lion, he stalks, plotting to make you his next victim. (See 1 Peter 5:8.)

The more clearly you see him in the Garden of Eden, the more quickly you can identify him when he appears in your own backyard with his nasty bag of tricks. Recognizing your enemy is the first step toward victory over him.

CHAPTER FOUR

Making the Choice

The forbidden fruit was hanging on a tree within reach. It was dazzling and luscious. Eve moved closer.

"I want it! And what could be so bad about just one bite? Adam said that God said we can't eat it, but God didn't say why. He just said no. And that handsome creature I talked to promised me there's nothing to worry about. He says I won't die if I eat it. In fact, I'll be more alive than ever. I'll know things I've never known before. I'll be just like God! How could that be bad?"

The decision Eve was facing in the garden of Eden was much more important than whether she should eat a piece of fruit.

1. What crucial choice was she making?

   Choosing to be selfish and put her desires above God

   When was the last time you faced a decision like hers?

Eve was not a rebel, for according to 1 Samuel 15:23, rebellion is sin, and she was not yet a sinner. What was happening to her? (See 1 Tim. 2:14 and 1 Cor. 11:3.)

She was rejecting God and becoming a sinner.

To Think and Talk About

Why do you think Satan chose to approach Eve first?

Satan used three classic weapons against Eve. He uses the same ones against you every day. They are named in 1 John 2:16: "For all that is in the world, the **lust of the flesh**, and the **lust of the eyes**, and the **pride of life**, is not of the Father, but is of the world."

To *lust* is to crave, to yearn, to ache for something, especially when it's off-limits. The lust of the flesh is the longing to satisfy the desires of your body. The lust of the eyes is the desire to possess something that pleases your sight but God has not chosen to give you. *Pride* is the arrogance that leads you to think that you that you can indulge those lusts without consequences. Watch how the devil uses lust and pride to deceive Eve.

> And when the woman saw that the tree was good for food, and that it was pleasant to the eyes, and a tree to be desired to make one wise, she took the fruit thereof, and did eat, and gave also unto her husband with her; and he did eat. (Genesis 3:6)

"And when the woman saw that the tree was good for food . . ."

The first thing Eve noticed was that it was a succulent fruit. As she gazed, her mouth watered and she just had to have a taste. She was facing the **lust of the flesh**—a longing for something that promises physical pleasure, something that is not lawful for us to have. Cheesecake looks even more scrumptious when we're on a diet. Leading men in the movies seem more handsome and virile than our own husbands. Television and sofa cushions call to us most loudly when there's a house to be cleaned.

2. What is your greatest fleshly (physical) temptation? How do you avoid giving in to it?

to be lazy - make lists and set goals of accomplishing tasks.

". . . and that it was pleasant to the eyes . . ."

Next Eve noticed the fruit's color and shape. Women love beauty, and this fruit must have been gorgeous. She was now experiencing the **lust of the eyes.**

3. What do you see and long for that others enjoy but that God has not provided for you?

What steps can you take to decrease the power of that lust over you?

Be content and thankful

". . . and a tree to be desired to make one wise . . ."

Remember the cheesecake? To your physical craving for that diet-forbidden treat, now add the sound of a soothing voice assuring you that eating cheesecake is good for a woman on a diet. In fact, the voice says, eating cheesecake will actually help you *lose* weight! You listen to the voice and imagine a skinnier you that everyone will admire. The **pride of life** kicks in and your brain says to your will, "Why not? It won't hurt you. In fact, it's the *right* thing to do!" It's hard to be tough on Eve when you imagine how hard it would be to withstand that triple-whammy attack on your appetite, imagination, and pride.

4. How has the devil been working on your mind lately? What twisted logic has he been using to attack your conscience and desire to obey God?

    ____

    ____

To Think and Talk About

Recall a time when you gave in to the temptation to sin, really believing that the end would be pleasure and peace. Is that the way things turned out? Which tools was Satan using on you?

If Satan was successful in deceiving Eve, who had no sin nature making her want to do wrong, what easy targets we are, for we are born with a bent toward sin. (See Rom. 5:12.) We are capable of doing wrong without one bit of help from Satan. But he and his evil angels still show up every day to offer us opportunities to sin. Watch out for Satan. He is not your friend; he is a fiend who has been perfecting his techniques of temptation since Eden. He has such confidence in his skill that he even tried them (without success) on Jesus Christ. (See Matt. 4:1–11.) He is using those wiles on you right now, hoping to make you his next victim.

> For we wrestle not against flesh and blood, but against principalities, against powers, against the rulers of the darkness of this world, against spiritual wickedness in high places. (Ephesians 6:12)

> Be sober, be vigilant; because your adversary the devil, as a roaring lion, walketh about, seeking whom he may devour: Whom resist steadfast in the faith. (1 Peter 5:8–9)

The GPS in our car has a wonderful feature: it warns me when I'm approaching one of those traffic cameras that snap pictures of cars running red lights. When I hear that beep, I might even stop on the yellow. I wish I had a GPS built into my brain to warn me when temptation is one block ahead so I could watch out for it. But I have something (someone) much better—a mighty God who lives in me to protect and deliver me from sin.

> But the Lord is faithful, who shall stablish you, and keep you from evil. (2 Thessalonians 3:3)

> The Lord knoweth how to deliver the godly out of temptations. (2 Peter 2:9)

> There hath no temptation taken you but such as is common to man: but God is faithful, who will not suffer you to be tempted above that ye are able; but will with the temptation also make a way to escape, that ye may be able to bear it. (1 Corinthians 10:13)

Sadly, Eve did not escape from Satan's temptation. She surrendered instead.

> She took of the fruit thereof, and did eat, and gave also unto her husband with her; and he did eat. (Genesis 3:6)

I wonder what Eve said as she offered Adam the fruit. She might have used the same logic Satan used with her, offering this evidence that the fruit wasn't lethal: "Look! I ate it and I'm still alive. Try it!" We don't know how the conversation went, but we know this: Adam was not fooled by either Satan or Eve. When he took his first bite, he knew exactly what he was doing.

> And Adam was not deceived, but the woman being deceived was in the transgression. (1 Timothy 2:14)

5. If Adam was not fooled, why did he eat the fruit?

Because he wanted it and chose his desires over God's desires

---

"You're not the boss of me!" That's what children sometimes say to their siblings. They aren't the first ones to talk that way. That's what Lucifer was saying to God in Isaiah 14:13–14, and it's what Adam was saying to God in the garden. "His sin was, in one word, disobedience, Ro[mans] 5:19; disobedience to a plain, easy, and express command. He had no corrupt nature within, to betray him; but had a freedom of will."[1] His choice showed "a love of self, dishonor to God, ingratitude to a benefactor, disobedience to the best of Masters—a preference of the creature to the Creator."[2] God clearly lays the blame for the first human sin on Adam.

> Wherefore, as by one man sin entered into the world, and death by sin; and so death passed upon all men, for that all have sinned. (Romans 5:12)

6. Who was the *one man*?

   Adam

   What two things came into our world the moment he disobeyed?

   sin and death (Separation from God)

   What sentence have we all received for his crime?

   Separation from God

That moment is called the Fall of man, for since then every human has been born with a sin nature. On behalf of all the rest of us, Adam forfeited perfection and became guilty before God.

In Adam's Fall,
we sinned all.[3]

To Think and Talk About

Your sin may not affect every generation after you, as Adam's did, but sin always hurts others. When *you* sin, who in your own small world is hurt? In what ways?

Adam's disobedience brought pain and death to all the rest of us. From him we all inherit a sinful nature, and because of that, we all choose to sin.

> As it is written, There is none righteous, no, not one. . . . They are all gone out of the way, they are together become unprofitable; there is none that doeth good, no, not one. . . . For all have sinned, and come short of the glory of God. (Romans 3:10, 12, 23)

7. Are you a sinner? yes According to Romans 6:23, what is the penalty due for your sin?

   yes! Death, separation from God!

Of course you will die physically, but this means much more than physical mortality. That is only the first death. Eternal death, or the second death, is eternity in a horrible place the Bible calls hell. (See Rev. 20:14–15; 21:8). But the good news is that "the gift of God is eternal life through Jesus Christ our Lord" (Rom. 6:23). On the cross, Jesus gave His innocent life to save you from the penalty due for your sin. He suffered the punishment for your sin and endured the anguish you deserve. In exchange, He offers you full forgiveness and eternal life.

> For he hath made him to be sin for us, who knew no sin; that we might be made the righteousness of God in him. (2 Corinthians 5:21)

To receive God's full pardon for sin and His gift of eternal life, sincerely pray a prayer like this:

> Dear God, I know that I was born a sinner and that I have chosen to do wrong. Because of my disobedience to You, I

> deserve only eternal death in hell. But I believe that Jesus died for me on the cross and took the punishment I deserve. Right now I turn from my sin, trust Jesus alone as my Savior, and ask You to save me from my sin and its penalty. Please give me your free gift of eternal life. I give you my life. Help me to live for You.

Salvation is as simple as that—turning from sin to the Savior! It is a step from darkness to light, and it is the first step toward having power over sin. Before salvation, we have only parental training and personal will power to resist doing wrong. But after salvation, we have the mighty power of God within us.

In His strength you can resist Satan's attacks. *Only* in His strength! Do not attempt to confront the Devil and his demons alone. Not even Michael the archangel did that.

> Yet Michael the archangel, when contending with the devil he disputed about the body of Moses, durst not bring against him a railing accusation, but said, The Lord rebuke thee. (Jude 1:9).

Instead take up the "shield of faith . . . to quench all the fiery darts of the wicked" (Eph. 6:16). Then wield the "sword of the Spirit, which is the Word of God" as your offensive weapon against his temptations (6:17), and the written Word empowered by the Holy Spirit will fight for you. The battle is the Lord's.

> Ye are of God, little children, and have overcome them [deceivers]: because greater is he that is in you, than he that is in the world. (1 John 4:4)

> The enemy is so securely entrenched within us that he can never be driven out while we are in this body: but although we are closely beset, and often in sore conflict, we have an Almighty helper, even Jesus, the Captain of our salvation, who is ever with us, and who assures us that we shall eventually come off more than conquerors through Him. With such assistance the new-born nature is more than a match for its foes. Are you fighting with the adversary today? Are Satan, the world, and the flesh, all against you? Be not

discouraged nor dismayed. Fight on! For God Himself is with you.[4]

CHAPTER FIVE

Bruised by the Fall

> This is the way God meant it to be before there was any sin in the world: sinless man, full of love, in his tender, strong leadership in relation to woman; and sinless woman, full of love, in her joyful, responsive support for man's leadership. No belittling from the man, no groveling from the woman. Two intelligent, humble, God-entranced human beings living out, in beautiful harmony, their unique and different responsibilities. Sin has distorted this purpose at every level. We are not sinless any more. But we believe that recovery of mature manhood and womanhood is possible by the power of God's Spirit through faith in His promises and in obedience to His Word.[1]

God's original plan was marvelous, intended to bring us perfect joy and satisfaction. But the moment sin entered the world, everything changed—for the worse. Now no matter how much we want to do right, we must struggle with sin. Even nature bears the scars of Adam's disobedience. But because there is a Redeemer, there is hope! Satan's doom is sealed, and all through eternity God will reign.

But as long as we live on this earth, we will have to deal with the enduring effects of the Fall. Understanding what they are will help you make sense of your world and of your own struggles.

Covering

The moment Adam and Eve yielded to temptation, Satan's prediction came true: their eyes were opened, and they knew good and evil. Conscience was awakened, and they were no longer innocent.

1. What was the first thing they knew? What was the first thing they did? (See Gen. 3:7.)

   they were naked so they covered themselves.

Before sin there was no need for shame, but as soon as innocence was gone, clothes became necessary. A woman once told me that since God created the female body to be so lovely, a woman should bare hers as much and as often as possible. (And she did!) She was right about the beauty of God's creation, but wrong about the rest. If we didn't need to wear clothes, life would be simpler . . . and much cheaper! But we do, because the Bible does not end at Genesis 2. God set a precedent for human modesty when He made clothes for Adam and Eve.

2. How did He do that? (See Gen. 3:21.)

   used animal skins

The sacrifice of animals to provide a covering for humans symbolized a later sacrifice—the death of a Redeemer to cover our sins. (See Isa. 61:10.) Clothing is a visible reminder that we are sinners. Before sin entered the world, Adam and Eve were naked but not ashamed. (See Genesis 2:25.) After sin entered the world, what did God call nakedness? (See Ex. 32:25; Isa. 47:2–3; Jer. 13:26; and Nah. 3:5.)

Avoid shaming yourself by what you wear (or don't wear), and you'll head off sin both in yourself and in others. When a woman willfully, knowingly dresses immodestly, she is saying, "I don't care how this affects you. It's my body, and nobody is going to tell me what to put on it." When a man looks at her with lust, he is actually saying, "I am going to use your body for my own pleasure." Both of these attitudes are rooted in the "lust of the flesh, and the lust of the eyes, and the pride of life" (1 John 2:16). Men and women are individually responsible for their own sinful choices.

Confrontation

3. What did Adam and Eve do next? (See Gen. 3:8.)

They hid from God

Why did they do this? (See Gen. 3:9–11.)

They were ashamed because they knew they were wrong and now knew they were naked.

During her toddler years when our daughter had disobeyed, she would stand very still with her eyes squeezed shut, thinking that if she couldn't see me, I couldn't see her. But of course I could. And no matter how much we try to hide from Him, God always sees us.

> For mine eyes are upon all their ways: they are not hid from my face, neither is their iniquity hid from mine eyes. (Jeremiah 16:17)

Since God is everywhere and knows everything, it's impossible to hide anything from Him. (See Ps. 139:1–12.) He already knew what had happened in His garden.

4. Why then would He ask the questions in Genesis 3: 9, 11, and 13?

So Adam and Eve would know what THEY had done. make sure they understand!

Why do you think he questioned Adam first?

leader to Eve.

Adam and Eve tried to hide, but God came looking for them, not in anger but in love, for He still wanted fellowship with them. He asked them several simple questions and let them choose to either make excuses or admit their guilt. Read Genesis 3:11–13 and think carefully about the next few questions before answering them.

5. Adam blamed Eve. Was she responsible? Why or why not?

   No. Everyone makes their own choices!

   Eve blamed the serpent. Did he deserve it?

   No. She chose to sin. He didn't force her.

My husband and I once watched a deaf couple arguing. It was easy to see that they were angry, but since they were using sign language, we couldn't tell what the argument was about. After seeing them repeatedly exchange the same vigorous sign, we asked an interpreter what it meant. He explained that they were saying over and over, "Don't blame me; blame yourself! Don't blame me; blame yourself! Don't blame me; blame yourself!"

Though your arguments may not involve using that sign, if you're like the rest of us, you're familiar with that scenario, for wherever there are human beings, there are conflicts. And in each conflict, there are people who are quick to blame others and slow to acknowledge their own guilt.

To Think and Talk About

> Eve had more of an excuse for her behavior than Adam did. (See 1 Tim. 2:14.) But neither was willing to accept responsibility. Who or what do women tend to blame for their own bad behavior? What about you? Where do you lay blame when you want to deflect it from yourself?

Curses

Even if they didn't want to accept liability for their bad behavior, the just judge pronounced His sinning creatures guilty and passed sentence. (See Gen. 3:14–19.)

On the Serpent

All creation, including both nature and animals, would now begin a long decay. But the serpent, whose body the spirit-being Satan had used, began to suffer immediately.

6. We're not sure what a serpent's posture and diet were like before the Fall, but what would they be now?

   Slither on its belly, eat dust of the earth

On Satan

The curse on Satan, the mastermind of evil, came next. The Devil hadn't planned on this. Since he had succeeded in getting them to obey him rather than God, "Satan probably believed that he had now won the allegiance of the first man and woman and therefore also of all their descendants. They would be allies of himself and his host of evil angels in their efforts to dethrone and vanquish God."[2]

But it didn't work out that way. God announced, "I will put enmity between thee and the woman and between thy seed and her seed" (Gen. 3:15). Eve, God said, would now understand that Satan was her enemy, and so would her seed. Everywhere else in the Bible, human posterity is called "the seed of the man," and that's biologically accurate. Only one child has ever been born as "the seed of a woman" with no human father.

7. Who was He? (See Isa. 7:14; Luke 1:26–35; and Gal. 4:4.)

   Jesus

According to 1 John 3:8–10, who are the seed of Satan?

Whoever does not practice righteousness or

does not love His brother

So now there is a continuing battle between good and evil: Jesus Christ and those in Him versus Satan and his followers. But Satan is going to lose this war. His end is sure: "It [the seed that is Christ] shall bruise thy head, and thou shalt bruise his heel" (Gen. 3:15). Satan bruised Jesus' heel when He died on the cross, and though His pain was dreadful, it was temporary. Three days later He rose again, guaranteeing eternal life for those who accept Him as Savior: "For as in Adam all die, even so in Christ shall all be made alive" (1 Cor. 15:22). But at the resurrection, Satan's power was broken, his head crushed, his final destiny sealed.

8. According to Revelation 20:10, what will eternity be like for Satan?

   lake of fire and torment day and night

   forever!

The announcement in Genesis 3:14 that a Savior would destroy the devil is called the *protoevangelium,* or the "first gospel." The promised Redeemer has come, and the gospel is complete. At the cross He paid the penalty due for our sin; every day He gives us power to conquer sin; and someday He will deliver us from even the presence of sin. What a glorious promise for those who accept Christ as Savior. Our battles with sin and Satan will end in victory. We are on the winning side!

> For this purpose the Son of God was manifested, that he might destroy the works of the devil. (1 John 3:8)

> And the God of peace shall bruise Satan under your feet shortly. (Romans 16:20)

On Women

Motherhood

But until our enemy's final defeat, women must carry the burdens passed down from Eve, who is called "the mother of all living" in Genesis 3:20.

9. We all know that motherhood is full of inexpressible joys, but how did the Fall affect pregnancy and childbirth? (See Gen. 3:16.)

pain in childbirth

And how does the Fall affect parenting? Our babies are precious, but very early they begin to show signs of the sinful self-will they have inherited from Adam through us. Their nature is to rebel against authority (otherwise known as Mommy and Daddy). Only by God's redeeming, sustaining grace, and years of patient training can we grown-up sinners raise our adorable little sinners to love and obey their Creator.

Marriage

The Creator's original blueprint for marriage—man as loving leader, woman as fulfilled helper—was a blessed and beautiful plan. But sin introduced selfishness to the earth, and so marriage became less a paradise than a battleground.

The struggles we confront in marriage were predicted in Genesis 3:15–16: "Thy desire shall be to thy husband, and he shall rule over thee." God warned that the peaceful relationship He intended for marriage would be disrupted by sin, as "the woman will now desire to 'have' her husband, just as sin crouched at the door, desiring to pounce on Cain."[3] (The same words for *desire* and *rule* are used in Genesis 4:7 for Cain's struggle with sin.) Even those who work diligently at having a marriage that follows a biblical pattern will find it tough, because a man's inclination to dominate rather than lovingly lead and a woman's tendency to resist rather than defer are strong in our sinful natures.

Sadly, in many cultures (even in some religions), women have been systematically subjugated and abused rather than cherished and protected. Even in Christian homes, a husband's leadership can be distorted by sin into harshness or cruelty. This is sinful, and it is never God's will. If you or your children are being abused in your home, quickly find help from the spiritual and legal authorities who have been entrusted by God with the responsibility to protect the innocent. (See Rom. 13:1, 4.) Don't stop looking until you find someone who will act in your defense.

But if you are blessed with a kind, good husband, praise God for the great blessings such a man's loving headship brings to his wife: "It produces the conditions essential to her work—order, coordination, protection, support, security, peace. It does not infringe upon her true liberty. It does not make her an inferior. It provides her with the ideal conditions in which she can display her character, use all her gifts, and fulfill her life."[4]

Relax and enjoy the 'ezer role God has written for you. Beware of the uprising of mutinous emotions that cause you to bristle at being the helper rather than the leader in your family, remembering that the unruly desires that cause you to press and maneuver until you get your own way are a result of the Fall.

To Think and Talk About

> What is the only limitation on a wife's submission to her husband's leadership (Acts 5:29)? How should a wife biblically handle this situation? when a husband asks a wife to go against God's law - God comes first!

All through Scripture, the Lord uses the unique intimacy of marriage as an illustration of His relationship with His own people. To the Jews He said, "For thy Maker is thine husband; the Lord of hosts is his name; and thy Redeemer the Holy One of Israel; The God of the whole earth shall he be called. For the Lord hath called thee as a woman forsaken and grieved in spirit, and a wife of youth, when thou wast refused, saith thy God" (Isa. 54:5–6).

This image extends even into eternity, for Christ's redeemed ones will be welcomed to their eternal home at the Marriage Supper of the Lamb. (See Rev. 19:9.) In John's vision of the future, when one of the seven angels presents all believers to the apostle John, he says, "Come hither, I will shew thee the bride, the Lamb's wife" (Rev. 21:9). Christ is the perfect groom; in heaven we who know Him as Savior will be (finally!) His absolutely perfect bride.

So God established marriage in the Garden of Eden. He is looking forward to welcoming us as His bride to His heaven someday, and today He watches over His institution by giving us clear guidelines for how to *do* marriage His way. Marriage is not just a private social relationship that we are free to define and live out however we want, making up rules to suit ourselves as we go along. It is instead, in the words of a very old wedding ceremony, "an honorable estate, instituted of God, signifying unto us the mystical union that is betwixt Christ and his Church."[5]

According to Ephesians 5:22–33, the headship and submission model of a godly marriage serves as an object lesson to the world.

10. What does it illustrate?

We need to submit to God - He will lovingly
and unselfishly lead - if we will follow

You and your husband have the amazing privilege of being a living sermon in your community, showing others through your marriage how much Christ loves His bride. When you relate to each other in a godly way, fulfilling your biblically defined roles in happy harmony, you are so dramatically different that others can't help but notice and wonder what your secret is. The joy you show in following His path will open hearts to hearing from you about the love of your Savior.

Can you see what is at stake every day after you say "I do"? Joyfully, willingly relinquish control to the God-chosen leader in your home. Live out your marriage the Lord's way, and you will give Him glory!

On Men

While the curse on the woman was connected to her relationships, the man's curse was linked to his responsibility as a provider. Read Genesis 3:17–19. Adam was already used to tilling and tending the ground.

11. But after the Fall, what was different?

 Man would have to labor to provide for his family

 How did this change life for Adam and every breadwinner, farmer, and gardener since?

 hard work! weeds, thorns, bugs!

To Think and Talk About

If there is a man in your life who has accepted responsibility for your welfare, he carries a heavy burden. What are his daily physical, mental, and emotional challenges? How can you lighten his load? Be an encourager to Him - help him provide - pray for him!

On Nature

Paradise on earth was over. Adam and Eve were exiled from Eden and blocked from returning by angels and a flaming sword. (See Gen. 3:24.) The earth began its steady decay. (See Heb. 1:10–11.) Now we have to dust, wash, weed, mend, and repair to keep our little worlds from falling apart. Our bodies weaken, wrinkle, sag, and will someday return to dust—despite all those vegetables, vitamins, lotions, potions, running, and lifting of weights. But someday—oh that blessed someday—the curse will be lifted from all creation, including you and me. What a day that will be!

> Because the creature itself also shall be delivered from the bondage of corruption into the glorious liberty of the children of God. For we know that the whole creation groaneth and travaileth in pain together until now. And not only they, but ourselves also, which have the firstfruits of the Spirit, even we ourselves groan within ourselves, waiting for the adoption, to wit, the redemption of our body. (Romans 8:21–23)

While we wait for our final deliverance, we can serve our Lord and do battle with our enemy. And we can enjoy living in His freedom right now, right here on earth. Even on our sin-cursed planet, if we're in Christ, life can be wonderful. And in heaven with Christ, home will once again be as perfect as it was in the garden.

To Think and Talk About:

Which results of the Fall are causing you the most trouble today?

Time for an Intermission . . .

The first three chapters of the Bible are packed with truth women need to know, since truth protects us from the lies that surround us.

Remember this. Our viewpoint as Christians is *theistic* (God-focused) while the world's perspective is *humanistic* (man-focused). We believe that God's Word is the absolute, infallible truth, while the world accepts as true whatever human notions are popular at the moment.

Here are some beliefs that I have found on anonymous Internet posts and carefully reworded. How would you biblically respond to each of them?

1. The Bible was written by a bunch of men who thought they were superior to women, so they made God a male. I'm female, and so I prefer a female God.

   Bible is God's Word - men were instructed by Him what to write.
   we were created in His image - He is the Creator - we are the Clay - He has full rule.

2. Since Adam was made first and Eve second, Eve obviously was his inferior and designed to be his servant.

   Eve was not inferior, designed to be his helpmeet, They were one, each helping the other

3. Husbands and wives need breathing space. Insisting on lifelong fidelity is unrealistic and can ruin a marriage. Some amount of sexual freedom is necessary and even beneficial. What society calls *adultery* is actually normal and no big deal.

adultery is sin! - not allowed at any time!

God is holy and cannot overlook sin of any kind!

4. The Bible is misogynistic [characterized by hatred of women], a souvenir of the gender war waged against women for thousands of years. It was written when intolerance for women's rights was acceptable because women were considered as inferior to men. Since we don't believe that anymore, the Bible is outdated, and we can ignore it.

Bible is never outdated and never changes

with society! The true word of God

5. Satan is a myth left behind by less enlightened eras, the embodiment of our fears, as unreal as a child's nightmare. He's a make-believe monster Christians dreamed up to scare people into church.

"He is as a roaring lion seeking whom he

may devour!" Real and wants us to follow

him rather than God!

6. Children are born innocent. The more they are left alone to develop naturally, the more creative, interesting adults they will become.

We are born into this ~~world~~ world w/a

sin nature. "As by one sin entered the world

and death by sin, so all have sinned!"

. . . and a Change of Scenery

Throughout the Old Testament, God consistently entrusted long-term family and national leadership to men. Several exceptional women spoke for God on a few occasions, but no woman was called by God to a long-term prophetic ministry, and no woman was inspired by God to write Scripture. Yet God insisted on respect for womanhood. The Ten Commandments demand equal obedience to both mother and father. In Proverbs, offspring who honor parents are called wise, while those who show contempt for the instruction of either parent are cursed.

Jewish women were equal participants with men in feasts and worship celebrations, and Christ came in preincarnate form to speak directly to some of them just as He did to men. Following Jehovah's instructions, the Jewish nation "held women in high esteem, honor and affection. . . . Under the Hebrew system the position of woman was in marked contrast with her status in surrounding heathen nations. Her liberties were greater, her employments more varied and important, her social standing more respectful and commanding."[1]

Sarah and Rebekah, for example, were strong and beloved women with positions of influence in their households. Jochebed's early training of Moses safeguarded his heart as he grew up in an Egyptian court; his sister Miriam worked beside him as he led the nation of Israel. Hannah's psalm of praise in 1 Samuel 2 shows remarkable insight into God's work and character. Through Esther's obedience, courage, and tactful wisdom, God preserved the Jews from destruction. King Solomon showed exceptional respect for the counsel of his mother, Bathsheba. His portrait of the ideal wife and mother in Proverbs 31—perhaps based on her life—is a classic tribute to the virtues of a godly woman.

God also used and honored non-Jewish women, even some from heathen lands. The Canaanite Rahab protected the spies from the wicked king of Jericho and was memorialized in Hebrews 11 as a model of faith. The Moabitess Ruth is honored as decisive, loyal, self-sacrificing, and pure. All through the Old Testament, courageous, believing women of all nations were protected and honored by God and by those men who lived to please Him. Abuse and exploitation of women are marks of pagan societies, not of those who live by the Book. Those who truly honor God also honor women.

When the New Testament opens in Matthew 1:3–6 with Christ's ancestry, we find women in the kind of genealogical list where the names of women rarely appear. From the many women among Christ's ancestors, the Holy Spirit chose to mention several with sad and even sinful life stories. One of them, in Genesis 38, seduced Judah by pretending to be a prostitute. In Joshua 2, we learn about the one who was a Gentile harlot. Another in the list was from a heathen Moabite background (Ruth 1). And 2 Samuel 11–12 tells of still another who committed adultery with King David, which led to the murder of her husband and the birth and death of her newborn son.

Including these women in Christ's genealogy reminds us that no matter what we have done, God can forgive us and transform our lives. The stage has now been set for the arrival of Jesus Christ, the Redeemer of both Jews and Gentiles. "Why does God include such dubious characters in the line of the

Savior? . . . These women are among the first hints that God's grace will explode, pouring out on the nations, opening the floodgates to rich and poor, slave and free, male and female."[2]

The next section of our study will be a refreshing change from the first one. In Act One, the first Adam yielded to Satan, leaving us an inheritance of condemnation and bondage to sin. In Act Two, the second Adam, Jesus Christ, arrives on earth's stage. He rises with healing in His wings. (See Mal. 4:2.) He conquers our enemy and sets us free from the curse of sin.

We're about to discover that our mighty Savior is also our matchless friend.

ACT 2

Woman in the Gospels

CHAPTER SIX

Made of a Woman— The Friend of Women

Jesus was born in Judea, a province of the Roman Empire. Though it's always risky to over-generalize social customs, there's no doubt that at the time of His birth, women faced serious restrictions in both social and religious life. The inferiority of women was not so much taught as simply assumed. "It is fair to say that a low view of women was common, perhaps even predominant before, during, and after Jesus' era."[1] We'll soon learn more about first-century customs, but for now remember this: though He did not come to be a social reformer and never directly taught on the topic, Jesus set an example of treating women with dignity. He never spoke harsh or degrading words to them. Instead He lifted their burdens and welcomed them as His disciples.

> The most striking thing about the role of women in the life and teaching of Jesus is the simple fact that they are there. Although the gospel texts contain no special sayings repudiating the view of the day about women, their uniform testimony to the presence of women among the followers of Jesus and to His serious teaching of them constitutes a break with tradition which has been described as being 'without precedent in [then] contemporary Judaism'.[2]

Made of a Woman

> But when the fulness of the time was come, God sent forth his Son, made of a woman, made under the law, to redeem them that were under the law, that we might receive the adoption of sons. (Galatians 4:4–5)

Just like you, Jesus was carried in His mother's womb. But unlike you, He had no human father. Conceived by "the power of the Highest" according to Luke 1:34–35, He was born to a virgin. His unique birth was a fulfillment of Isaiah's prophecy: "Therefore the Lord himself shall give you a sign; Behold, a virgin shall conceive, and bear a son, and shall call his name Immanuel [God with us]" (Isa. 7:14).

The Messiah could have arrived as a fully grown man and made a spectacular, dazzling entrance onto earth's stage. But He didn't; He arrived as we all arrive.

1. Why do you think the Trinity planned such a simple advent for the Son?

   ____

   ____

In a world that valued kings and emperors, soldiers and philosophers, wealthy and wise men much more than ordinary women, a young woman (probably a teenager) from a simple village was chosen to give birth to the Son of God. Joseph was an honorable man who, though he played no part in Jesus' conception, protected the infant and served Him well as His earthly father. But it was Mary who experienced the incomparable mother-son bond with Jesus from the hour she laid Him in the manger until she stood near His cross.

Mary was the true physical mother of the incarnate Son, but she cannot accurately be called "the mother of God," for God is eternal. He has no beginning and will have no end. Mary never claimed nor was given an exalted place among His disciples or special privileges in the early church. She knew her only honor came from what God had done for her: "Behold, from henceforth all generations shall call me blessed. For He that is mighty hath done to me great things; and holy is His name" (Luke 1:48–49). Mary simply loved Christ as His mother and served Him as His disciple. But still—what a privilege she was given!

In the incarnation, Jesus was humbled (see Phil. 2:5–8), but womanhood was exalted. By being born of a woman, by being carried in Mary's arms and choosing to be obedient to her (see Luke 2:51), Jesus paid tribute to the joys and burdens of motherhood.

To Think and Talk About

> In our joys and trials, mothers can either bring God glory or focus on themselves. Can you think of some motherly actions and reactions that are self-centered rather than God-centered?

The physician Luke told the stories of Mary and her cousin Elizabeth in Luke 1–2. He described their emotional and spiritual responses to their miraculous pregnancies as well as the physical facts of the births of Jesus and John. Obviously some of these are unique to them (though every baby is a miracle), but others are common to every mother and may be familiar to you.

The particulars of pregnancy and delivery are usually much more interesting to females than to males. (Watch men squirm in embarrassment when women share too much information.) But everything mattered to God, from Mary's need for specifics about her baby's conception to how she wrapped Jesus after His birth, from John's leaping in Elizabeth's womb to the decision about his name. I don't know how many weeks their morning sickness lasted or how many hours of labor they endured, but I can assure you that the Father does, for He notices all a mother goes through as she carries and cares for her child.

During His ministry it was necessary for Jesus to establish independence from His mother and other family members. In passages such as Luke 2:49, John 2:1–11, and Mark 3:31–35, He makes it clear that His love and respect for His immediate family members and even His compliance with His mother's sincere, well-motivated requests for His help were secondary to His calling to do the will of His Heavenly Father. His words and actions also pointed out the truth that no physical act (even giving birth to the Savior) or human relationship guarantees personal salvation. Only the new birth into the family of God through repentance and faith brings redemption. Mary understood this, for she acknowledged her need of a Savior in Luke 1:47.

But even as Jesus suffered on the cross, He showed special concern for His mother's needs. (See John 19:25–27.) What an encouragement and example He is for those of us who care for aging parents.

All women can praise Jesus Christ for the honor He gave us through His incarnation. Since the birth of its founder, one mark of genuine Christianity has been esteem for motherhood, and for that we praise Him.

To Think and Talk About

> Does Mary's mothering of Jesus extend into eternity? How did she see herself in relationship to Him when she was on earth? Is it biblically right to worship Mary or ask her to intercede for us? (See Luke 1:46–48 and 1 Tim. 2:5.)
> one mediator and that is Jesus Christ ↑

A Friend of Women

The sisters Mary and Martha and their brother Lazarus were Jesus' special friends. (See Luke 10:38–42 and John 12:2–3.) Their home in Bethany was a place for Jesus to retreat from the crowds that thronged Him begging for help, a place to eat and talk to a family He loved. Friends share life by sharing time. But the best friends do even more.

> Iron sharpeneth iron; so a man sharpeneth the countenance of his friend. (Proverbs 27:17)

2. How does a true friend *sharpen iron*?

by checking in with them spiritually and sharing scripture to encourage them to keep putting God first!

Jesus was the best friend Mary and Martha could have had, because He challenged them to grow in their faith. You're probably already familiar with their story.

3. While Jesus and His disciples visited in their Bethany home, where was Mary? Where was Martha?

at Jesus feet worshiping Him. Martha was busy serving and preparing food.

Mary demonstrated the posture of a disciple—the place of humility before a teacher. Just as Paul learned the Jewish law "at the feet of Gamaliel" according to Acts 22:3, Mary was sitting at her Master's feet, learning truth from the one who is called "the truth" in John 14:6. That wasn't the customary place for Jewish women, who ordinarily were not taught by the rabbis. The more usual place for a woman was serving at home as Martha did. (And it's a good thing, or there would have been no dinner.) But rather than rebuking Mary, as the overworked Martha expected, Jesus praised her. It's a classic story with many applications, but let's focus on this one: in contrast to other religious teachers of His day, Jesus accepted a woman as His disciple. He commended her desire to learn at His feet, and He challenged Martha (and the rest of us) to do the same.

> But one thing is needful: and Mary hath chosen that good part, which shall not be taken away from her. (Luke 10:42)

To Think and Talk About

What makes it hard for you to spend time sitting at Jesus' feet? What practical steps can you take to make it easier?
Selfishness - phone calls

We meet the sisters again in John 11. The message they sent Jesus was as concise as a text message—no details! (See John 11:3.)

4. What does this brief communication reveal about their relationship to Jesus?
They trusted in Jesus and knew He loved them.

Mary and Martha seemed sure He would rush to their side, but He didn't. In fact, He delayed His coming so long that He missed Lazarus's funeral by four days. They were openly and understandably disappointed that He did not come sooner. In John 11, Jesus gently deals with the grieving Martha, using her sad experience to strengthen her faith.

Just as Jesus arrived in Bethany, Martha came out to meet Him. (See John 11:20.) Read her first words to Him in John 11:21–22.

5. By what name and title did she address Him?
Lord

In what tone of voice do you think she spoke the words in John 11:21?
disappointingly sad.

What did she already know about Jesus? (See John 11:22.)
He could have kept Lazarus from dying.

Martha's Christology (the doctrine of the person of Christ) was correct. So was her eschatology (the doctrine of things to come), for when Jesus promised in John 11:23, "Your brother shall rise again," she agreed that was true.

6. But when did she expect his resurrection? (See John 11:24.)

   When he went to Heaven to be with God

Jesus, of course, knew that Lazarus's resurrection would come much sooner than that, so He turned her focus from some uncertain "last day" of resurrection to Himself.

7. What theology did He teach her in John 11:25–26?

   That in believing in Jesus, ye could have eternal life

Then He asked her this very simple question: "Do you believe this?" But instead of answering with a yes or no, she spoke from her heart an amazing truth.

8. What was it? (See John 11:27.)

   She believed that Jesus was the Son of God

This is a remarkably full and clear confession of faith, one that even most of Jesus' disciples couldn't have stated so clearly. (Peter was one exception in Matthew 16:16.) It's our creed too; it's been the doctrine of the church since the days of the apostles. Martha understood exactly who Jesus was. But it's obvious that she had still more to learn about the power of God the Son.

9. When Jesus called for the stone to be rolled away from the grave, what was she expecting? Or not expecting? (See John 11:39.)

   to see Lazarus' dead body decayed

Instead of an embarrassing stench, out came her brother—alive! What an incredible, faith-strengthening moment! I wish I could have seen her face. Surely in that instant, belief in the power of the Messiah moved from her head down into the deepest places in her heart.

> Martha believed in the power available to Jesus Christ; she believed that if He had been there He could have healed her brother; she also believed that Jesus had a special intimacy with God, and that whatever He asked of God, God would do. But—she needed a closer personal intimacy with Jesus. Martha's theology had its fulfillment in the future. But Jesus continued to attract and draw her in until her belief became an intimate possession. It then slowly emerged into a personal inheritance—"Yes, Lord, I believe that You are the Christ . . ." (John 11:27).[3]

To others Martha may have been "just a woman," but Jesus, knowing that her faith was genuine, used her pain as a means of bolstering her faith. If you're in emotional pain right now, have you considered that maybe it has come because the Lord sees holes in your faith that He wants to fill? Have you been set aside from your normal activities for a while by physical sickness? Maybe He has moved you out of the whirlwind of life because He longs for you to sit at His feet.

> I would witness to the fact that the deepest, the most precious, and the most abiding spiritual lessons which God has been pleased to teach me were learned in consequence of enduring my various experiences of sickness. This . . . is particularly true in respect to the prayer-life, the praise-life, the life of dependence upon God, and the life which chooses to live not for the seen, but for the unseen, not for the temporal, but for the eternal . . . I feel it would have been nothing short of a calamity to have missed the physical suffering through which I have passed.[4]

Jesus didn't see Martha or Mary as inferior to His male disciples. "Christ's attitude was one of full and open fellowship with them in spiritual things."[5] Just as He longed for them to sit at His feet, just as He wanted them to believe in Him more deeply, He also desires your fellowship and wants your faith to grow. He was a true friend to these sisters. He is your friend too.

To Think and Talk About

> When the Lord wants your faith to move from your head to your heart, which is His more effective tool—pain or joy? Why? When has this happened to you? How did you respond to what He was doing?

CHAPTER SEVEN

Women Serving Christ—Christ Serving Women

As we follow Jesus' footsteps through the Gospels, we see Him living out this truth: "There is neither Jew nor Greek, there is neither bond nor free, there is neither male nor female: for ye are all one in Christ Jesus" (Gal. 3:28).

Jesus allowed believing women to serve Him, and He in turn was their willing servant.

Women as Jesus' Servants

Supplying Needs

1. Read Luke 8:1. What was Jesus doing?

   Spreading the Gospel

   Who was with Him?

   His disciples and several women

The twelve disciples were His closest companions. He lodged with them; He taught, tested, and mentored them.

2. Who else was in this group of travelers? (See Luke 8:2–3.)

   Mary, Joanna, and Susanna and others

Some of these women were wealthy and prominent, but others had neither fame nor riches.

3. What do you think motivated them to follow and serve Him?

Jesus had helped them with their infirmaties (problems)

What needs would they have provided out of their own means?

Women at that time did not have means to provide for themselves except their husbands

The word used in Luke 8:3 for *ministered* means to wait on as a servant. This was a ladies' traveling missionary society—one with big, open purses!

4. Why was their help necessary? (See Luke 9:58 and 2 Cor. 8:9.)

Provide for Jesus and their disciples

As Creator and Sustainer of all things (Col. 1:14–17), Jesus could have miraculously and continuously provided anything He and His followers needed. But instead He let these women provide for them.

5. Why do you think He chose to live that way?

To prove that God can provide for us and to show God can use anyone for His purpose

To Think and Talk About

You were born too late to help supply Jesus' needs as He traveled in Galilee. But you can still serve Him "out of your substance." How? Giving back a portion of His money, time - to witness, help others, pray, study God's word

Standing By

Most of the disciples had run away from the scene of Jesus' crucifixion in justifiable fear, but many women were there, including Jesus' mother Mary, who with the beloved disciple John stood close enough to the cross to hear Him speak to them. (See Mark 15:40–41 and Matt. 27:55–56.)

> When Jesus therefore saw his mother, and the disciple standing by, whom he loved, he saith unto his mother, Woman, behold thy son! Then saith he to the disciple, Behold thy mother! (John 19:26–27)

Crucifixion would have been a horrible sight even if you didn't know the one suffering. But these women stayed near the cross as Jesus died, though they knew they could do nothing to stop His illegal, bloody execution. The depth of the women's agony, as they stood helplessly watching their innocent Lord and friend suffer, is hard to fathom.

6. So why were they there?

Because they loved Him

After His death, while the disciples hid from the threat of arrest by the Romans, several women were still bravely serving their Master.

7. What did they do? (See Matt. 27:59–61; Mark 16:1–2; and Luke 23:55–56.)

Watched and were ready to help anoint His body with spices to show their respect

Jesus accepted the service of women not because He was a male who thought He deserved to be waited on by females, but because He recognized that they believed on Him and loved Him. The job of being a servant in God's kingdom is open equally to men and to women.

Women Jesus Served

Here's an even more amazing truth: Jesus Christ, God the Son, came to earth not to be served but to serve. The Creator of all men and all women came to earth as our humble servant.

> Even as the Son of man came not to be ministered unto, but to minister, and to give his life a ransom for many. (Matthew 20:28)

To Think and Talk About

> Many religions worship false gods who make harsh demands on their followers who want to gain acceptance and avoid punishment. How is our Master different?
>
> He wants to help us! He does not need our help!

Whenever destitute, suffering, neglected, or downcast women came near Jesus, He went out of His way to find them and offer His help. After solving their immediate problems, He presented these needy women as examples of faith to others who thought themselves superior, moving them from dark obscurity onto the bright pages of the Gospels. Let's meet a few of them.

A Disabled Woman in Luke 13:10–17

Jesus was teaching in a synagogue where as a rule, women worshipers were segregated from men. As Jesus began to speak, He noticed, standing nearby, a woman with a terrible problem.

8. What was wrong with her?

   disabled by an evil spirit (Bent over)

Though she had not come to ask for help, Jesus took the initiative and changed her life with one simple announcement: "Woman, thou art loosed from thine infirmity" (13:12). Immediately she stood up straight—for the first time in eighteen years! Wouldn't you have cheered? Or wept in joy?

But the leader of the synagogue and others, according to 13:17, were aggravated and irritated instead. Jesus had interrupted His sermon, spoken directly to a woman, and invited her into a group of men, and they were annoyed with Him for breaking their religious rules. Even worse, He, like any good physician with a patient, had touched this woman—another appalling breach of their manmade law. (See Luke 7:39.) The ruler of the synagogue couldn't see past the broken rules to the miracle taking place right in front of his eyes. Jesus had just shown Himself to be God with power over demons and disease, but all the religious leader could do was gripe.

9. What particular bone did he decide to pick with Jesus (13:14)?

   why did He do it on the Sabbath - there are

   6 other days to work.

In the Old Testament Law, God had established Sabbath rules such as taboos on profit-making work and other distractions to rest and worship. But some activities were allowed, such as any labor essential to protecting life or to showing mercy on living creatures.

10. What example—very familiar to the men in the synagogue—did Jesus mention (13:15)?

   taking their animals from food to a place

   to give them water.

Jesus pointed out that they cared more about their donkeys than about this poor woman, also a Jew, who had been afflicted by a demon for almost two decades. She was a suffering human being, of much more value than a thirsty animal. I'm relieved to read that the grumblers began to be ashamed and that soon many people loudly rejoiced over Jesus' healing miracle. That day, in that synagogue, Jesus ignored the fault-finders, exposed their hypocrisy, and raised the status of every suffering woman.

An Afflicted Woman in Mark 5:21–34 and Luke 8:40–48

Jesus and His disciples had just arrived by boat on the northwest shore of the Sea of Galilee. A multitude of people seeking His help had gathered, but a prominent synagogue ruler named Jairus got His attention first. He fell at Jesus' feet, begging Him to heal his dying twelve-year-old daughter. A ring of anxious disciples tried to hustle Jesus toward Jairus's house, while a mass of people were "pressing Jesus so that he could hardly move because of the jam, or even breathe."[1]

Abruptly, Jesus stopped the procession and asked what must have seemed an absurd question: "Who touched me?" People were so crammed together that everybody was touching somebody else whether they wanted to or not. But this touch was different.

11. Who had laid her hand on Jesus' garment? What was her problem? (See Mark 5:25–28.)

a women with a blood disorder for 12 years

This was most likely chronic menstrual bleeding, one of those uniquely female problems that can be embarrassing to talk about. When this Bible story came up in a conversation, a friend confided to me, "I once bled constantly for months. It was awful, and I was mortified to tell anybody about it, even to ask them to pray for me." It is touching and encouraging to realize that Jesus Christ, the Creator of the female body, cares about its special infirmities. He understands the inconveniences and challenges of our cycles and hormones. No problem is too awkward to bring to Him in prayer; nothing we endure is beyond His loving compassion.

This woman had spent every penny she had trying to find a cure for her humiliating problem, but Mark 5:26 says that all the doctors had done was to make her even sicker. So now she wasn't only ill, she was also destitute. And lonely, too, for her disease made her ceremonially unclean. Read Leviticus 15:19–27 to discover why she would have been shunned by her law-keeping neighbors, who would have been fearful of spiritual contamination as well as repulsed by her bloody hemorrhage. She would also have been banned from synagogue and temple worship. For a dozen years she had been literally untouchable.

12. But what happened when she touched the hem of Jesus' garment? (See Mark 5:29.)

    immediately she was healed!

    What happened to Jesus at the same moment? (See Mark 5:30.)

    He felt His power leave Him and asked who touched His garment.

    Of course, Jesus knew who had touched Him and why, for He knows everything about everybody, so why did He ask the question when He already knew the answer?

    So she would come forward so all could see and hear!

He drew this "fearing and trembling" (Mark 5:33) woman out of isolation to offer her as a model of faith. Her quivering account in Luke 8:47 of what had just happened brought glory to the Great Physician. And when He said in front of her townspeople, "Daughter, be of good comfort: thy faith hath made thee whole; go in peace" (Luke 8:48), He brought her great honor. How tenderly He treated her, even addressing her as *Daughter*—the only time He referred to a woman by that title.

What a change! Before her healing, even one touch from her was enough to contaminate others, so they avoided her. It took only one touch of the hem of the Master's garment to make her both completely clean and confident of His love. Though her disease had robbed this poor woman of all but her faith in Christ, faith was all she needed.

By the time Jesus got to Jairus's house, his daughter was dead. But Jesus waded right through the mob of wailing mourners to the bedside of that little girl—and resurrected her! That's another moment I wish I could have seen. Jairus's crisis was well-known in their community, but the need of one anonymous woman in the crowd was no less important to Christ. No one is invisible or untouchable to our Lord. How tender He is to every woman who endures physical suffering.

A Burdened Woman in Matthew 15:21–28

The woman in the last story came meekly, but this one came boldly, even audaciously. Why? It's because the help she so desperately wanted was for her child. Every mama can identify with that.

13. What was wrong with her daughter (15:22)?

posessed by a demon

She was a Canaanite, not a Jew. But she called Jesus "the Son of David" and "Lord" and worshiped Him (15:22, 25).

14. Why would she do that?

She believed He could help her daughter and believing He was the Son of God.

Why were the disciples annoyed (15:23)?

She was being loud and distracting.

This distraught mother came to Jesus, believing Him to be the Messiah, determined to get His attention and persuade Him to heal her suffering child. She didn't care whom she embarrassed, including herself. It's a fascinating scene, because Jesus seems a bit rough on her.

15. What did He do at first (15:23)?

Sounded like He was turning her away.

Then what reason did He give for not helping her (15:24)?

She was not an Israelite (or a believer)

But she didn't give up! Like my friend who took her son to doctor after doctor—at great expense and despite some criticism—until she found an accurate diagnosis and cure for his illness, this woman persevered. Even when Jesus seemed to reject her pleas, saying that He couldn't "take the children's [Jews'] bread, and cast it to [Gentile] dogs" (15:26), she didn't give up. She begged for just a few crumbs of help, and He gave what she needed, in abundance. Her daughter was healed.

Jesus was not being callous by making her beg for help. He was challenging her to show the extent and depth of her faith. Didn't He already know what was in her heart? Of course He did. And He also knew all along that He was going to heal her daughter. But He wanted her to demonstrate her resolute faith to His disciples as a living illustration of the kind of unwavering belief He longed to see in them.

Have you ever prayed desperately for God to restore someone you love who was suffering from serious sickness or the bondage of sin? I've been there. I know how hard it is to keep on praying with the assurance that God does hear and care when He is silent. I know what it is to beg for God for help *right now* when He seems to be working much too slowly. I know what it is to ride the roller coaster of faith-doubt-faith-doubt-faith-doubt-faith-doubt until I'm dizzy and nauseated. That's why I love this woman's story. This mother did not know that Jesus *would* help her. She just knew that He—and only He—*could*. So she asked, asked, and kept on asking.

Are you now pleading with Him to help, to heal, to fix someone you love who's broken? Ask, ask, ask, and keep on asking, despite the delay, despite your doubts, even when all you have faith to ask Him for is a few crumbs. He is always at work, even when you can't see anything He is doing in answer to your prayers.

When the wait seems interminable, you cannot see what He is doing, and you wonder if He even hears you, by faith believe that He is even then at work for you. While you are anxiously focusing on your one fervent desire, He is actively working together a multitude of details—all for your good.

Keep praying. God will answer. And when He finally does, you will hear Him (and me too) say, "O woman, great is thy faith!"

To Think and Talk About

> One of the women Jesus healed didn't even ask for it. One wanted help from Jesus but not the attention of others. Another did not care one bit what others thought and would not leave until He met her need. Jesus helped them all. What does this teach us about our Lord? About prayer?

What a friend we have in Jesus,
All our sins and griefs to bear!
What a privilege to carry
Everything to God in prayer!
Oh, what peace we often forfeit,
Oh, what needless pain we bear,
All because we do not carry
Everything to God in prayer!

Have we trials and temptations?
Is there trouble anywhere?
We should never be discouraged—
Take it to the Lord in prayer.
Can we find a friend so faithful,
Who will all our sorrows share?
Jesus knows our every weakness;
Take it to the Lord in prayer.[2]

CHAPTER EIGHT

Women with Sorrows—Women with Regrets

We are about to meet two women whose private lives needed redemption. They had each suffered the death of a woman's most precious relationships. One was not responsible for her losses, but the other likely had destroyed them herself. Seeing how Jesus helped them will encourage you that regardless of your present predicament or past failures, He sees you not as you *are* but as you *can be,* and that He is willing and able to transform you. He is the peace your troubled heart longs for; He is the truth that can set you free; He is the source of a new and abundant life.

A Bereaved Woman in Luke 7:11–17

Luke tells us yet another story of a mother weeping for a child. This child wasn't just sick; he was dead. As Jesus entered the city of Nain, He and the group with Him met a crowd accompanying a young man's coffin to the cemetery.

1. Why was his death an especially severe blow for his mother? (See Luke 7:12.)

   She was a widow and no other sons to provide for her.

Among the Jewish people, the death of an only son was seen as a reason for bitter sorrow and lamentation. In fact, Old Testament prophets used it as a metaphor for great calamity.

> O daughter of my people, gird thee with sackcloth, and wallow thyself in ashes: make thee mourning, as for an only son, most bitter lamentation: for the spoiler shall suddenly come upon us. (Jeremiah 6:26)

> And I will turn your feasts into mourning, and all your songs into lamentation; and I will bring up sackcloth upon all loins, and baldness upon every head; and I will make it as the mourning of an only son, and the end thereof as a bitter day. (Amos 8:10)

For a widow, the death of her only son was devastating. Unless someone offered her charity, she would be reduced to begging, since in that culture there was no way for a woman alone to support herself.

2. When Jesus saw this weeping mother, what did He feel? What did He say? What did He do? (See Luke 7:13–15.)

Compassion. Don't cry. Told the man to "get up"

The man got up and spoke to Jesus!

In the margin of my Bible near verse 15, I have written, "WOW!" This young man sat up, spoke, and climbed right out of his coffin. In an instant, a mother's weeping was turned to laughter and her mourning to elation. One day earlier, Jesus had healed the servant of an influential Roman army officer, but the grief of this poor widow was no less important to Him. "No sorrows of a Christian mother, especially a widowed mother on the death of an only son, escape the tender and sympathizing notice of the Savior. His bosom swells with pity. . . . He [was] preparing to pour into her wounded spirit the balm of consolation and cause the desolate, sorrowing heart to sing for joy."[1]

I have a son in heaven who died before birth. Maybe you also have a child waiting there for you. We will see them again!

But this woman was able to hold her living son again on earth, and the moment his life was restored, so were her hopes.

Maybe your child is still alive physically but because of rejection or sinful choices seems dead to you. Believe this, because it's true—God is able to resurrect that treasured relationship and restore your beloved child. He does what no one else can do.

If you are a widow, be encouraged by this story. God sees you. He knows your needs and cares about them.

3. What did the Law say about how widows and orphans were to be treated? (See Ex. 22:22–23.)

   We are not to mistreat them. If you do - judgement will come to your wives & children.

   What does God promise widows? (See Deut. 10:17–18 and Ps. 146:9.)

   Watch over them and lift them up and execute justice for them.

Maybe you are a different kind of widow—a woman physically or emotionally abandoned by your husband. The man who pledged himself to your welfare has deserted you instead, leaving you to provide for yourself and your children. His infidelity has broken your heart, and even worse, damaged your ability to trust again. If that's true of you, open God's Book and read Romans 8:31–39 as His message to you.

4. In this passage, what gifts does God promise you?

   never to leave us - nothing can separate us from God's love!

   He is our conqueror!

   What protections does He offer?

Which of your fears do these promises put to rest?

If everything fails us - we Always have God who is all powerful and has a perfect plan for us!

Memorize this passage. Meditate on it. Live in it with the confidence that the Savior of the widow of Nain is your Savior too. He sees your tears and knows your pain. At this very moment, He is at His Father's right hand praying for you. No one can steal His heart from you, for He is totally committed, absolutely faithful, and will never break a promise. He cannot lie. He will never, never, never forsake you (Heb. 13:5). The God of all comfort will comfort you (2 Cor. 1:3) and the Father of the fatherless will care for your children (Ps. 68:5).

While they were in exile in foreign lands, the nation of Israel suffered like a wife rejected by her husband. God said to them: "Fear not; for thou shalt not be ashamed: neither be thou confounded; for thou shalt not be put to shame: for thou shalt forget the shame of thy youth, and shalt not remember the reproach of thy widowhood any more. For thy Maker is thine husband; the Lord of hosts is his name; and thy Redeemer the Holy One of Israel; The God of the whole earth shall he be called" (Isa. 54:4–5).

If you are a woman left alone by death or abandonment, that promise is for you!

To Think and Talk About

Because He was "despised and rejected of men; a man of sorrows, and acquainted with grief" (Isa. 53:3–4), our Messiah knows how to share our heartaches. Do you know someone in pain because of bereavement, an estranged child, or a broken marriage, whose heartache you could share? How can you help carry her burdens?

Pray!

A Sinful Woman in John 4:1–42

John 4 is a classic soulwinning chapter. If you want to learn how to meet a stranger, open a conversation about what matters most, and lead a soul to salvation, this is the passage to study, for here we watch the Savior lead a thirsty soul to the "well of water springing up into everlasting life" (4:14). But there are also other lessons to learn from this chapter.

As the story opens, we learn that while traveling with His disciples from Judea to Galilee, Jesus "must needs go through Samaria." There were other routes He could have taken, but He chose this one so that He could keep a divine appointment. There was a woman He needed to meet, something He needed to say to her, something for His disciples to learn through their meeting, and a city to evangelize. John 5:30 tells us that Jesus came to do His Father's will, and it was the Father's will for Him to meet this woman in this place.

As they traveled, Jesus and His disciples came to an isolated spot near the city of Sychar. They likely had started their trip at sunrise, and by this time they were weary, hungry, and thirsty. While the disciples went into the city to buy food, Jesus sat by the famous well of Jacob and waited for a woman He knew would arrive. She came alone, which was unusual, for a walk to the well to draw household water was a customary time for women to socialize. Maybe she was being shunned by decent folks—and maybe for good reasons.

She expected to also be snubbed by the man sitting by the well. She could see by His appearance that He was a Jew, while she was a Samaritan. Samaritans were related to Jews, but old racial, political, and religious conflicts between them had hardened into a proverbial enmity. (In John 8:48, a group of Jews used these words to insult Jesus: "Thou art a Samaritan, and hast a devil.")

Since the woman at the well expected contempt from a Jew, she was shocked when Jesus spoke to her. But she was intrigued enough to open a conversation: "How is it that thou, being a Jew, askest drink of me, which am a woman of Samaria?" (John

4:9). And there was another reason for her to be surprised that He spoke to her: it was simply that she was a woman. It would have surprised anybody who saw that scene.

> And upon this came his disciples, and marvelled that he talked with the woman. (John 4:27)

"There was a rabbinical precept: 'Let no one talk with a woman in the street, no, not with his own wife.'"[2] And this was not just an ordinary woman; she was a *sinful* woman. She had had five husbands already and was now living in adultery with a sixth man.

5. What do you think had happened to the first five? What are all the possibilities? Which do you think is most likely? How would those experiences have affected her?

   They left the relationship because there was really no relationship or love. No commitment!

To Think and Talk About

> It's becoming increasingly common for unmarried couples to cohabit. Is just living together, even in a long-term committed relationship, the same as marriage in God's eyes? What did Jesus say about it in John 4:17–18? Considering the laws of both God in Genesis 2:24 and man in Romans 13:1 and Titus 3:1, what is necessary to biblically establish a marriage?

The woman at the well had lost husbands, friends, and reputation. She had had a hard life already, and the future didn't look any brighter. Even before their first greeting, Jesus knew all about her sinful past, but He had a plan to redeem her from it all. To talk to this adulterous Samaritan woman, He had to break local social and religious rules, and He crossed them boldly, not for shock value, but for His divine purpose.

Nor was He there to discuss religious differences between the Jews and the Samaritans, though she brought up that subject in John 4:19–20. Since they were excluded from the Jerusalem temple, the Samaritans worshipped at Mt. Gerizim instead. Their worship was worthless, according to Christ, because they did not know God (4:22). But Jesus was not at the well to convince this woman to worship in a different place. He was there to offer her new life.

To this anonymous, sinful woman in a wilderness place, Jesus made two dramatic announcements.

6. What was the first announcement in John 4:21–24?

   That it didn't matter where you worshipped - only to the one true God!

   The new worship was not to be sacrifices made in a mountain or temple, but in hearts, "in Spirit and in truth."

   What was the second announcement in John 4:25–26?

   Christ was coming - the Messiah - and He was the Christ!

Jesus did not often make such a plain declaration of who He was. A literal translation of His statement in John 4:26 is, "I who speak to you am." He was identifying Himself as the Old Testament Jehovah, the great "I AM." It was such an unambiguous claim to be God that when He said the same thing to the Jews in John 8:58, they tried to stone Him as a blasphemer.

What a striking scene—Jesus the Messiah sitting by a well teaching theology to one adulterous woman. But He chose His audience well, for she listened carefully, believed His words, and instantly became His wholehearted servant.

If we had decided to launch a citywide evangelistic crusade in Sychar, we would have gone about it in a different way—organizing disciples into committees, leasing a hall, renting folding chairs, raising funds for publicity, scheduling special music, training a choir, and more. But the Lord needed only one changed life to transform a city. She was so excited that she left her water pot behind (like forgetting your purse) and ran straight back into the streets of her city with her news: "The Messiah, the Savior of the world, has come!" I suspect that she was not a bit timid about it.

> And many of the Samaritans of that city believed on him for the saying of the woman, which testified, He told me all that ever I did. (John 4:39)

The Lord chose the most unlikely (and maybe the most unliked) person in town to be a home missionary. Only our Savior can transform a life like this. He didn't just save her from her sin; He gave her a new calling and a purpose higher than fulfilling the lusts of men. She undoubtedly had to bear painful private scars and a damaged public reputation all the rest of her life, for sin always leaves us worse than it finds us, and we cannot eradicate the past. But when salvation comes, so does a new life, for "if any man be in Christ, he is a new creature: old things are passed away; behold, all things are become new" (2 Cor. 5:17).

I met a lovely young woman while I was speaking at a women's retreat. When Emily was introduced to me as a newlywed, I thought that must be the reason for her shining face—but I soon learned the real source of her joy.

"I'm Emily," she said, "but not the Emily I was two years ago. I'm brand-new! You won't believe how different I am now. I can hardly believe it myself. Let me tell you what God has done for me!"

She quickly summarized a past of sinful choices and addictions of all sorts, a life of such desperate hopelessness that she was on the brink of suicide when an acquaintance invited her to her church's addictions-recovery group.

"Why not?" she thought. "Nothing else has worked. Maybe this will."

And it did! There she was introduced to Jesus Christ, who saved her soul and transformed her life. He banished her guilt with His forgiveness and replaced her turmoil with His peace. He gave her a purpose and a reason to live, and then brought into her life a pure, godly, loving husband.

"And now," she concluded, "I tell everybody—and I mean everybody—about my Lord! How could I ever keep quiet about what He has done for me?"

Many have been pointed to Jesus through the contagious joy and bold testimony of Emily, a modern Samaritan woman.

To Think and Talk About

> If you have a history of failure, you may have believed you are disqualified to serve the Lord today. *He saved me*, you might think, *but He saved me too late*. Or you may know another woman who believes this about herself. How has the story of the Samaritan woman altered your thinking? How can the Lord use the story of your redeemed past to help others?

7. Compare Luke 7:16 to John 4:41–42. What was the final outcome of both these stories?

   they believed!

God can—and does—take the most wretched circumstances, the kind that crush our spirits and rob us of hope, and give them new meaning. He can—and does—bring Himself glory by showing Himself powerful over our problems. He can—and does—comfort the brokenhearted and restore the fallen. Only God can do that—but He does!

Another Intermission

The Savior of the world is the friend of women. As we read the Gospels, we watch Him go out of His way to notice and meet the needs of women of varying social standings, ages, and races. He even used the routines of a woman's life to illustrate spiritual truth. For example, He once told a story about a woman sweeping her house for a lost coin and celebrating when it was finally found. He took a scene we're all familiar with—"Where's my cell phone? Where are the keys? Has anybody seen my sunglasses? Hooray, I found them!"—and with it created a memorable illustration of His seeking for sinners and of the "joy in the presence of the angels of God over one sinner that repenteth" (Luke 15:10).

When Jesus wanted to portray the quiet power of the gospel and how quickly it would multiply in hearts, He used this image familiar to his listeners: "The kingdom of heaven is like unto leaven, which a woman took, and hid in three measures of meal, till the whole was leavened" (Matt. 13:33). Jesus must have watched His mother adding leaven to meal as she baked bread and then drawn on that memory as He taught. These simple illustrations not only made sense to any woman listening; He invited everyone into her kitchen to learn kingdom truths.

And Jesus openly censured practices that led to the abuse of women. For example, He exposed the hypocrisy of a group of Jews who wanted to publicly stone a woman caught in adultery while concealing their own mental infidelity. (See John 8:3–11 and Matthew 5:27–30.) He also confronted the twisted laws that permitted men to divorce their wives on a whim. (See Matthew 5:31–32.) Imagine living in a community where your husband could discard you for minor faults or just because he was bored and then hearing Jesus insist on a man's unwavering commitment to his marriage vows. What a friend Jesus was to women!

Of course, Jesus' offer of salvation and friendship did not exclude men. He never set women above men in any way, but He consistently lived out this truth: in His family, there are no gender distinctions.

But while there is no inequality in our *standing* in Christ, there is diversity in our *function* within His Body, the church. There is no difference in *who we are,* but there are differences in *what we do.* "His free and merciful attitude toward women introduced a revolutionary reappraisal of them. Their spiritual privilege was equal with that of men; definite differences, however, existed in their spiritual activity."[1] The section we're about to begin about women's role in the early church will help you understand and appreciate those differences.

Another Change of Scenery

In Act Three, our setting changes to the book of Acts and the Epistles so we can observe the role of women in the early church. Acts is a thrilling record of the first days of church history, starting with the return of Christ to heaven after His resurrection and the dramatic arrival of the Holy Spirit and ending about three decades later. It's a transitional book. Things happen in Acts that had never happened before and haven't happened since.

The twenty-one books that follow Acts, ending with Jude, are epistles, or letters. Most are written to local churches. As you read them, imagine you're back in the first century listening with other believers as a letter from an apostle like Paul, Peter, James, or John is read aloud. The writer refers to some of you by name (praising some, fussing at others), applauds your church's strengths, points out your weaknesses, and teaches you how to handle relationships within your church.

Many women are mentioned in Acts and the Epistles. Although they lived in the first century, those women were not that different from you and me. They also knew and loved Christ and wanted to please Him. Let's sit beside them and listen to what the Lord, through His inspired Word, says to us about our role in our twenty-first-century churches.

ACT 3

Woman in the Church

CHAPTER NINE

Leaders in the Church

Jesus treated women well, but as soon as He died and the apostles were in charge, women were demoted to second-class disciples. The leaders of the early church assigned leadership roles to men because they were typical women-haters. Within a century, women had lost the equal standing Jesus had given them, and unfair discrimination against women is still practiced in churches today. (Paraphrased from an anonymous Internet post.)

Are you shocked? Don't worry. I didn't write this, and I don't believe it! But others do. You can find opinions like this scattered across the Internet, and they come from sources both inside and outside of Christian churches. People who write such things believe that the writers of the New Testament (especially Paul) abandoned Jesus Christ's original intentions to impose their own social prejudices on local churches. Is that true? Let's find out.

First, be sure you understand the biblical meaning of the word *church.* In New Testament Greek, *ekklesia* often refers to an individual assembly of believers like the one you attend. But it can also mean the complete *body of Christ* (Ephesians 5:29–30), which is made up of all believers of all times. The context of the word makes its meaning clear.

1. For example, which *church* is referred to in Ephesians 5:25?

the complete body of Christ.

In 2 Corinthians 1:1?

individual church

To Think and Talk About

How does a person become a part of the body of Christ? Salvation
How does a person join your local church? Can you be part of one and not the other? Are you a member of both? yes

The Example for the Church

There's a foreshadowing of church life in the ministry of Jesus. Matthew 10:2–4 tells us the names of His twelve called and commissioned disciples.

2. Were there any women among them?

no

What were these disciples appointed to do? (Matt. 10:1, 5–8)

win the Jews to salvation and He gave them power to heal the sick

Jesus also chose of group of seventy men to travel and minister in His name, with assignments and duties similar to those of the twelve. (See Luke 10:1–16.) Though there were a great many women among Jesus' disciples, He delegated those specific tasks only to men.

The Founder of the Church

3. Who established the church? You'll find the answer in Matthew 16.

Jesus Christ!

___

___

People speculated about Jesus' identity in Matthew 16:13–16, but what did Peter know?

that He was Christ, the Son of God!

___

___

He was right, and Jesus said so in Matthew 16:17. How did Peter know this?

Because God revealed it to him!

___

___

Then in Matthew 16:18 Jesus declared that He was going to build something new. In this announcement, Jesus made a play on words: "Thou art Peter [*petros*: a little rock], and upon this rock [*petra*: a large boulder] I will build My church." Peter may have been just a pebble, but the truth he had just spoken, that Jesus was "the Christ, the Son of the living God," would become the solid-rock doctrinal foundation of the church.

This is the only time the word *church* appears in the Gospels. Though the church was still in the future, Jesus was already calling it *my church*. The concept and design of the church were His. He was its source and is still its head. By the time the first church congregation was established on the day of Pentecost in Acts 2:41–42, Jesus was alive at the right hand of His Father with all creation, including the church, subject to Him.

> According to the working of his mighty power, which he wrought in Christ, when he raised him from the dead, and set him at his own right hand in the heavenly places, far above all principality, and power, and might, and dominion,

> and every name that is named, not only in this world, but also in that which is to come: and hath put all things under his feet, and gave him to be the head over all things to the church, which is his body, the fulness of him that filleth all in all. (Ephesians 1:19–23)

Christ is the chief cornerstone of the church, which He has built on the foundation of truth spoken by men like Peter, men called to be His apostles and prophets.

> Now therefore ye are no more strangers and foreigners, but fellowcitizens with the saints, and of the household of God; and are built upon the foundation of the apostles and prophets, Jesus Christ Himself being the chief cornerstone; in whom all the building fitly framed together groweth unto an holy temple in the Lord: in whom ye also are builded together for an habitation of God through the Spirit. (Ephesians 2:19–22)

The Keeper of the Church

Jesus is continuously at work in and for His church. Ephesians 5:23–29 is a fascinating passage that compares His love for the church to the love of a husband for his wife.

4. How is the church related to Christ? How is He related to her? (See 5:23.)

   It is His bride. The head of the Church.

   What is the church's responsibility to Christ? (See 5:24.)

   Submit to Christ.

   What has Christ already done for the church? (See 5:25.)

   He has loved us and died for us!

What is He now doing for the church? (See 5:26.)

leading us to purity to exemplify true love.

What is His ultimate purpose for the church? (See 5:27.)

to stand before God purified + w/o blemish (sin)

The founder of the church, the one who calls Himself her loving, committed bridegroom, did not at His return to heaven abandon His apostles to figure out for themselves how to take care of His bride. He promised them that the Holy Spirit would come to be their teacher, to guide them as they led His work on earth. The Spirit arrived just in time for the founding of the first church in Jerusalem. (See Acts 2.)

> These things have I spoken unto you, being yet present with you. But the Comforter, which is the Holy Ghost, whom the Father will send in my name, he shall teach you all things, and bring all things to your remembrance, whatsoever I have said unto you. (John 14:25–26)

Another of the Spirit's tasks was to inspire the writing of the Bible. That's why we call it "God's Word."

> Knowing this first, that no prophecy of the scripture is of any private interpretation. For the prophecy came not in old time by the will of man: but holy men of God spake as they were moved by the Holy Ghost. (2 Peter 1:20–21)

> All scripture is given by inspiration of God, and is profitable for doctrine, for reproof, for correction, for instruction in righteousness. (2 Timothy 3:16)

5. So when we find instructions in the New Testament about how the church is to be led and governed, whose directions are they? Who will hold us to account for how well we follow them?

   God's direction. God will hold us accountable!

Church government is an issue of biblical accuracy, not of political correctness or social trends.

The Leaders of the Church

The Bible uses several different words for God's appointed leader of a local church, who has a high calling and solemn responsibility before God. The first word is *episkope,* translated in 1 Timothy 3:1 as *bishop.* A bishop is not the exalted name of a high church official, but a simple title given to one who supervises and manages, administrates and superintends the church.

Another word is *presbuteros,* or *elder*. "These two terms, bishop and elder, are often used interchangeably (Acts 20:17, 28; Titus 1:5–9). The former term (bishop) speaks of his office responsibility, while the latter term (elder) refers to his spiritual maturity."[1]

The third word is the one we're most familiar with—*pastor*. You'll find it in Ephesians 4:11, where the Greek word is *poimen,* or *shepherd.* When you call the leader of your church your pastor, you are using the Latin word for *shepherd.* The apostles used it too.

6. What did Peter say to other shepherds in 1 Peter 5:2?

watch over their people-willingly

And what did Paul tell them to do in Acts 20:28?

Care for the people as the Holy Spirit guides.

Sheep need shepherds because in general sheep aren't very bright. My Granddaddy Horne allowed his ten children to raise any animal on their family's mountain farm except sheep, because he said, "Sheep are *way* too much trouble!" Christ is our Chief Shepherd, Good Shepherd, and Great Shepherd, but pastors are His undershepherds. I'm afraid that we sheep cause our pastors way too much trouble, but they are patient with us though they have little earthly reward for all their work. Maybe that's why there's something special waiting for them in heaven.

7. What is it? (See 1 Peter 5:1–4.)

unfading crown of glory!

To Think and Talk About

A biblical pastor has not chosen a profession; he has answered God's call. What burdens are unique to his life? What sacrifices? What temptations? What do you think are the most common misconceptions the members of your church have about your pastor?

1 Timothy is a pastoral epistle, one of the three New Testament books (along with 2 Timothy and Titus) written to train a pastor in the details of leading a church. As we read these books, inspired by God Himself, we discover how a God-pleasing church functions.

1 Timothy 3:1–7 is packed with the qualifications and responsibilities of a biblical pastor.

8. Read these verses carefully and list the details that require a bishop/elder/pastor to be male. Some of these are repeated in Titus 1:6.

above reproach, one wife, not violent, not quarrelsome, not lover of money, manage his household well, submissive children.

Now find in 1 Timothy 3:8–13 the reasons that deacons, who are servants in the church, also should be men.

they are to be husbands w/a (one) wife that has a good reputation

So when a church restricts the offices of pastor and deacon to males, is the church guilty of chauvinism?

no, just following God's plan for the church

> It is . . . very important to understand that the Bible's ascribing different roles to men and women does not constitute sexism. The Bible makes it abundantly clear that God expects men to take the leadership role in the church and the home. Does this make women inferior? Absolutely not. Does this mean women are less intelligent, less capable, or viewed as less in God's eyes? Absolutely not! What it means is that in our sin-stained world, there has to be structure and authority. God has instituted the roles of authority for our good. Sexism is the abuse of these roles, not the existence of these roles.[2]

Today women serve as leaders in law and politics, business and industry, education, the arts, and science. There are almost no limits to our professional opportunities.

9. So why is a "glass ceiling" acceptable in the church?

There is one other instruction given in this epistle that—if we are committed to obeying God—restricts the role a woman can play in church leadership.

10. What boundary is set in 1 Timothy 2:11–12?

they are to be submissive to leadership. Not the leadership.

Read these verses in the context of the purpose of this letter—to teach the young pastor Timothy how to conduct church life—and you'll understand that this restriction is for church gatherings where men are present, rather than to women's Bible studies or children's classes. Since teaching God's Word is a position of spiritual authority, teachers of doctrine in mixed company are to be men. It is the elders (always male) who are to be the teachers (1 Tim. 3:2) and leaders (1 Tim. 5:17) of the assembled church. Paul gives Timothy two reasons for this: the order of creation and woman's vulnerability to the deceits of Satan. (See 1 Tim. 2:13–14.)

Don't be confused by the mention in 1 Corinthians 11:5 of a woman who "prayeth and prophesieth." Praying is talking to God, and there is certainly no gender restriction on that. Prophesying is teaching God's Word. Women have full freedom to do this in the right setting, and there are many contexts where it's appropriate and fully blessed by God. The four daughters of Philip the evangelist mentioned in Acts 21:8–9 were likely teachers of individuals or in acceptable settings within their church. Always interpret scriptures like this one in light of the clear instructions given in the epistles for church assemblies, such as 1 Corinthians 14:34–36 and 1 Timothy 2:11–12.

To Think and Talk About

> The church needs ministers, and since some women have speaking and leadership gifts, why can't we use them as pastors or teachers in mixed groups? Are we permitted by God to do everything we are capable of doing? What happens when women press to fill leadership roles God has not planned for them?

I have spent my life in the homes of two men in full-time ministry—my dad and my husband. Both of my sisters, many relatives, and most of my best friends are married to men in ministry. I have observed these men up close and can assure you that they take their calling seriously. While watching them deal with the heavy responsibilities that come with their calling, I've often given thanks that I am a woman! I don't envy their spiritual office. They face complex challenges as they work to handle God's business well, and they will be held by God to a high standard.

> My brethren, be not many masters, knowing that we shall receive the greater condemnation. (James 3:1)

The God-called men who lead your church have burdens that the women in the pews can help them carry. Our job is not to compete for theirs, but to follow them as they follow God, to pray for their protection from their unique temptations, and to obey the Scriptures they carefully teach. When we commit ourselves to fulfilling our biblical role in the church, we make it easier for them to fulfill theirs.

> Remember them which have the rule over you, who have spoken unto you the word of God: whose faith follow. (Hebrews 13:7) Pray for them.

> Obey them that have the rule over you, and submit yourselves: for they watch for your souls, as they that must give account, that they may do it with joy, and not with grief: for that is unprofitable for you. (Hebrews 13:17)

To Think and Talk About

This lesson began with this paragraph:

Jesus treated women well, but as soon as He died and the apostles were in charge, women were demoted to second-class disciples. The leaders of the early church assigned leadership roles to men because they were typical women-haters. Within a century, women had lost the equal standing Jesus had given them, and unfair discrimination against women is still practiced in churches today.
(Paraphrased from an anonymous Internet post.)

Develop your own biblical response.

CHAPTER TEN

Praying, Belonging, Serving

If women cannot scripturally serve as pastors or deacons in local congregations, then what *can* we do? More than we have time for! Let's look into the book of Acts and the Epistles to discover the pattern set for us by women in the early church.

We Can Pray

For forty days after His resurrection, Jesus appeared to many of His followers at different times and in different places. He talked to them and showed them His wounds; He ate and drank with them. There was no doubt that He was alive. Jesus promised His disciples that the Holy Spirit would come to be with them. The Spirit's power would fall, and as a result they would be bold witnesses "in Jerusalem, and in all Judaea, and in Samaria, and unto the uttermost part of the earth" (Acts 1:8). Then Jesus ascended to heaven, and the disciples were left alone.

They gathered in the upper room where they had celebrated their last Passover meal with Jesus, the room where the women had arrived fresh from the garden tomb to tell the disciples about the resurrection, the room where Jesus Himself had appeared to prove their story true. There they waited for the Spirit to come.

1. Which men were there (Acts 1:12–14)?

   the disciples

Joining them were Mary the mother of Jesus and other women. We don't know for certain who the others were, but it's likely that Mary Magdalene, Joanna, and Mary the mother of James had come (Luke 24:10), along with Mary the wife of Cleopas (John 19:25). Peter and some of the other apostles were married (1 Cor. 9:5), so maybe some of the wives had arrived with their husbands.

2. What was this group doing (Acts 1:14)?

   praying together

This was not a public worship service, but a gathering of men and women with equal standing before God for prayer. I love the phrase "with one accord" in verse 14. These believers were praying *unanimously*. I have sweet memories of a time like this when my husband and I met often for prayer with a church planter and his wife in their home. With one heart and mind, in "one accord," we asked for God's blessing on the new church about to be planted. As the Lord sent them, other men and women joined us to pray in unity and harmony toward our common goal.

To Think and Talk About

In your own church, when is it appropriate for you to pray publicly? When do you defer to men? Why? A careful study of the words of 1 Timothy 2:8 will help you understand the standard practice in many of our churches.

We Can Be Active Church Members

About three thousand people were saved and baptized the day the church was born, the day of Pentecost. (See Acts 2:41.) Those men and women became members of the Jerusalem church.

3. What were they all busy doing? (See Acts 2:42–47.) And you thought your church calendar was full!

teaching, fellowshiping, praying, providing for each other, and praising God

We're told that soon there were five thousand men on the church roll (Acts 4:4), along with many, many women, as "believers were the more added to the Lord, multitudes both of men and women" (Acts 5:14). They were baptized, "both men and women" (Acts 8:12), and diligently studied the Scriptures (Acts 17:11–12). The Lord even allowed women of the early church the privilege of serving Him in another way.

4. What happened to some of the women who were part of the Jerusalem church? (See Acts 8:1, 3.)

they were put in prision like the men.

There have been eras when women were not allowed to *own* property but were instead considered to *be* property. Even in our own country, women were not allowed to vote until 1920. Still today there are nations where a woman cannot drive, reveal her face in public, or choose her husband. But in God's kingdom, women are full citizens. Male or female, rich or poor, young or old, every believer can and should be an active, involved member of a Bible-believing congregation. The Lord welcomes you, and the rest of us need you.

We Can Serve

Positions of Trust

First-century church women served the Lord in significant ways in their churches. Of the twenty-six people Paul commends in Romans 16, eight are women. There's Phoebe (her name means *radiantly bright*), whom Paul met when he lived and worked in Corinth. In Romans 16:1–2, Paul calls her both his sister in Christ and a servant of the church in Cenchrea, a city near Corinth.

5. What did Paul ask the church in Rome to do for her? Why?

   Welcome her in the church. She supported Paul and other believers and provided for them

   How could a woman like Phoebe help Paul and the pastor and deacons in her church carry the burdens of leadership?

   Offer food or a resting place

Because he asks them to "receive her" (provide room and board), it's likely that Phoebe was a church guest, perhaps even the courier who delivered Paul's letter to the Roman church. That was a serious responsibility.

6. What positions of trust do women hold in your church?

   Sunday school teachers, preyer warriors, and helpers in others ministries.

Paul set a pattern that I have seen followed in the churches I have been a part of. Godly men in leadership speak generous words of praise for women who serve as Phoebe did. They pray for them and offer both spiritual guidance and practical help for their ministries. Like Paul, these men never belittle or downplay their role in the biblical church family. Instead, they honor women as beloved sisters and partners in Christ's service.

Physical Labor

In Romans 16:6, we meet a woman named Mary. Paul says she "bestowed much labor on us." The word used here suggests that she had served her church so fervently that she was exhausted or, as we say in my native South, "plumb wore out."

7. How do women use their physical energy serving in your church?

   Clean the church, food for Sundays, food for special assistance, and helping the homeschool group.

The sisters Tryphena and Tryphosa (maybe twins) we read about in Romans 16:12 also labored in their church. Their names mean *delicate* and *dainty*, so it must be possible to be feminine even while working hard.

Nurture

The anonymous woman Paul greets in Romans 16:13 was almost certainly Rufus's birth mother, not Paul's.

8. So why would Paul call her his mother?

   She probably cared for him as if he was her son.

This passage reminds me of a dear friend whose hugs and encouraging words, especially since my own mother's death, always leave me feeling loved and mothered. She is a praying, nurturing friend not only to her own family, but to everyone who knows her.

9. Who are the motherly women in your congregation? What makes them fit that description? How does their loving care benefit your church?

   they pray for everyone and inquire about them.

We get a glimpse into the ministry of older widows in 1 Timothy 5:9–10.

10. How did these women serve the Ephesian church?

showed hospitality and served others.

You may have heard of Tabitha, whose Greek name was Dorcas, which means *gazelle*.

11. What did she do for the people of Joppa, especially the widows? (See Acts 9:36–42.)

made clothes for them and did other many good works for them.

Dorcas could sew, and she found ways to serve others with needle and thread. Do you have an ability that seems sort of homely to you but could be used to bless others? Maybe you aren't musical but can do mending. You may not know what to say to a grieving woman, but you do give great hugs. Maybe you can't teach a Sunday school class but would enjoy baking homemade bread for lonely shut-ins. Maybe you can no longer take care of children in the church nursery but could deliver a family dinner to a tired mom. Ask Him to use your skills to cheer and support others, and He will show you how.

Evangelism

What touches me the most about Dorcas's life is not her good deeds, but what happened after her resurrection: "And it was known throughout all Joppa; and many believed in the Lord" (Acts 9:42). Her sewing brought aid to the poor, but her testimony brought salvation to many. And that is, of course, what really matters.

When Paul was greeting his friends near the end of his letter to the Philippians, he mentioned other "women which labored with me in the gospel" (Phil. 4:3). These coworkers *contended* with him; they *toiled* with him. They were his fellow workers, his colleagues in spreading the gospel, and they were women.

12. How can the women of your church work alongside its leaders to spread the glorious news of salvation to the lost?

SS teachers, VBS, music ministry, special assistence ministry, assist in any of the church ministries, and pray!

Don't be satisfied with just helping people physically when their greater need is spiritual. Be bold with truth. Souls hang in the balance. Do battle for them!

To Think and Talk About

> Why do most women find it easier to serve by cooking, cleaning, teaching children, keeping the nursery, or singing in the choir than to take an active part in evangelism? What does this say about our priorities? that is their role at home. They do it every day. We do what is comfortable. Sharing truth requires boldness.

Stewardship

Women can also use their homes to serve the Lord. My husband and I have spent most of our ministry planting new churches. Women who are willing to open their homes for gatherings are vital to a baby church whose meeting place may be available only on Sunday mornings. I have watched women cheerfully get their houses ready for company every Sunday evening and Wednesday night (and other times in between). They willingly store hymnals and folding chairs in the coat closet, set up a bedroom for child care, and make sure one bathroom is reasonably clean. Those who do this week after week, "heartily, as to the Lord, and not unto men" (Col. 3:23), are my heroines.

Such superwomen have been around for a long time. Since the early church began under persecution, illegal in the eyes of the government, it was two centuries before congregations were able to own property. Until then, they met wherever they could. The church at Colosse met in the home of Apphia and

Archippus. (See Phil. 1:2.) The church at Rome began in the home of Priscilla and Aquila. (See Rom. 16:3–5.)

13. What was happening in the home of Mary, John Mark's mother, in Acts 12:12?

    they gathered there to pray.

    How did the Lord use Lydia to help with the founding of the church at Philippi, the first church in Europe? (See Acts 16:11–15, 40.)

    She opened up her home to the believers to worship

Hospitality to Christian servants is so important that there's a whole book of the Bible about it. Here's the key passage of that short letter.

> Beloved, thou doest faithfully whatsoever thou doest to the brethren, and to strangers; which have borne witness of thy charity before the church: whom if thou bring forward on their journey after a godly sort, thou shalt do well: because that for his name's sake they went forth, taking nothing of the Gentiles. We therefore ought to receive such, that we might be fellowhelpers to the truth. (3 John 1:5–8)

That last sentence ought to encourage you to be a willing hostess. When you welcome servants of the Lord into your home and in friendship offer them comfortable beds and tasty food, you are encouraging them along their journey in a way that pleases God. You are becoming a colaborer in their work for the Lord wherever they are, as surely as if you traveled to Africa, Asia, or Europe to work beside them. What a privilege it is to serve God's servants through hospitality.

To Think and Talk About

Have you been treating your home as a private castle or a place for ministry? How can you use your guest room, your dining room, your back yard, your kitchen table, and your living room as tools to serve Christ?

CHAPTER ELEVEN

Learning, Sharing, Living

Learning the Word for Yourself

To be a disciple of Jesus Christ, a woman has to know His Word. To know it, she has to study it. To be an obedient disciple, she will share what she has learned with others. Studying the Word is a Christian woman's pleasure and privilege. Teaching what she has learned is her honor and obligation.

In Acts 17, Paul and Silas were in Thessalonica doing what God called them to do: telling the gospel story to people who had never heard it. When serious persecution began, the believers sent them by night to Berea, where they started preaching once more.

1. But what was different in Berea? (See Acts 17:11.)

they were soaking in the Word of God.

Who was among this *noble* group who not only listened carefully, but also studied the Scriptures meticulously every day to be sure that what they were hearing was true? (See Acts 17:12.)

many Greek Women

Be a Berean woman! Study God's Word for yourself. Know it so well that you can tell truth from error. Compare anything you hear from the pulpit or on the radio, everything you read online or in books, with His Book. That's our responsibility as women of God. Not so we can get filled up (and puffed up) with how much we know. Not so we can become known as walking, talking Bible encyclopedias. And not so we can teach men. (See 1 Tim. 2:12.) The purpose of learning the Word is to know God and then to make Him known by sharing what we have learned. We are not supposed to preach in church services, as we have learned. But we have the privilege of teaching truth in other settings.

Sharing the Word with Other Women

> The aged women likewise, that they be in behavior as becometh holiness, not false accusers, not given to much wine, teachers of good things, that they may teach the young women to be sober, to love their husbands, to love their children, to be discreet, chaste, keepers at home, good, obedient to their own husbands, that the word of God be not blasphemed. (Titus 2:3–5)

2. According to these verses, who's supposed to be teaching the younger women in your church?

the older women

What are the prerequisites for being a teacher of other women?

act holy, not accusers of others, not drinker, teacher of good behavior

What "good things" are we supposed to teach?

things that please God!

Why? So that husbands will be happy, children well-behaved, and houses neat? What is the higher purpose?

that God's word would not be defamed or get a bad name

Women have a natural bent toward creating and preserving relationships. We like to make new friends; we cherish our oldest, deepest friendships. We can use this God-given strength as we edify our sisters and daughters in Christ, whatever our age. I was a very young pastor's wife when I told a friend that I was glad to be off the hook on this Scripture, because I wasn't an older woman. She responded with this quiet question, "Do you know *any* women younger than you?" I got the point. We're not supposed to wait until we're old and wrinkled to share what the Lord has taught us. Helping other women grow in their walk with Him is not just a good idea; it's our scriptural obligation to accept this role and commit ourselves to it.

Teaching others doesn't mean you have to set up a class, assign homework, and give tests. This is certainly not a mandate to schedule yet another meeting in the church building. Think of it instead as a ripple effect, with your "behavior as becometh holiness" touching other lives in a way that spreads on and on, even to others you may never meet. See it as a private ministry. Come alongside a younger woman who is right now where you were not so long ago, facing decisions and difficulties that you have already come through. Guide her gently, lovingly through life's mazes with the wisdom you have gained from experience.

Mostly, think of it as giving her yourself as a gift: your ears to patiently listen as she pours out her heart, your mouth to speak gentle encouragement from Scripture, your heart to empathize and comfort. To be a teacher of younger women requires being both a good example and a trustworthy counselor, but most of all it means to be aware and available.

To Think and Talk About

In your church, who needs your teaching? How can you offer to help younger women without being pushy or preachy? Or maybe you are one who is longing to be helped and taught. How can you find a godly mentor? What happens in a church when the older women neglect their responsibility to be "teachers of good things"?

Living the Word Within the Church

One of my favorite first-century women is Priscilla (or Prisca), a woman who had remarkable influence in several early churches. She's an amazing "actress" in the drama of the book of Acts, one of the best models in Scripture of how a woman can serve God through His church while living within His guidelines. Her name is mentioned six times in Scripture, beginning with Acts 18:1–4.

We don't know when Priscilla first heard and believed the gospel, but when the Roman emperor Claudius banished the Jews from Rome about AD 50, she and her husband Aquila left their Italian home together to move to the Greek city Corinth. That would have been a long trip by boat and a challenging change in culture. They may have been members of the church in Rome—we're not sure—or perhaps they came to Christ later. The word *together* sets the tone for all we know about this couple, for they are always mentioned as a pair. (My husband speculates that this "A & P" started a chain of grocery stores, but I'm not sure he's right about that.) They worked together in a tentmaking enterprise. My own speculation is that this couple probably didn't have children, but that God's plan was for Priscilla's life to be fruitful in a different way.

Tents weren't just for camping back then, and they weren't made of ripstop nylon. Necessary to Jewish life, they were created from rough, heavy goat hides. To cut and sew tents took muscle and skill. Soon another tentmaker, the apostle Paul, arrived from Athens and began to help them. We don't know how they met, but we do know that Paul had not come to Corinth just to set up a business. He had arrived with something much more valuable than his leather-working tools: the life-altering gospel of Jesus Christ. Every Sabbath Paul preached to both Jews and Greeks in Corinth, reasoning with them and persuading them to believe in Christ.

3. What happened in Acts 18:8?

   Crispus (ruler of synagogue) and his entire family

   believed + were baptised

Soon there was a congregation in Corinth that included Priscilla and Aquila.

4. What role do you think this couple played in that baby church? How could Priscilla have helped the women in that wicked city? How could she have assisted Paul in his pastoral ministry?

   He could help teach the men and Priscillia could

   teach the women according to scripture and not their false religion and be future missionaries like Paul

Think what it would have been like for Priscilla and Aquila to have Paul sharing their life. They didn't just get to hear the apostle preach in the assembly; they worked beside him all day. At home, they shared quiet evening meals, where they likely learned firsthand the fresh truths that God was steadily revealing to him. They soon came to share Paul's courageous, contagious enthusiasm for the spread of the gospel. After eighteen months in this private Bible college, Aquila and Priscilla sailed for Ephesus with Paul (Acts 18:18–21), where he left the couple behind while he traveled to visit other churches. They probably once again set up a tentmaking business in a rented shelter near the marketplace. They worked at their trade and looked for opportunities to share truth.

One Sabbath while Paul was away, they heard Apollos preaching in the synagogue.

5. What do we learn about Apollos in Acts 18:24–25?

He was sincere & and dedicated to preaching

the Gospel accurately on John's Baptism - didnt understand death & resurrection

Apollos was a disciple of John the Baptist, the forerunner of Jesus Christ, and he preached John's doctrine of "the baptism of repentance for the remission of sins" (Mark 1:4). Red flags went up for Aquila and Priscilla as they listened to Apollos eloquently preach from the Old Testament. They could tell he believed in Christ as Messiah but didn't grasp the significance of His death and resurrection, the arrival of the Holy Spirit, or the beginning of the church. Apollos, they knew, was not an enemy of the gospel but a man who needed a fuller understanding of it. Instead of rebuking him publicly or criticizing him quietly, they made a wise decision.

6. What was it? (See Acts 18:26.)

took him aside privately to explain

instead of rebuking him publicly

Notice the *they* in this verse. Equally and privately, husband and wife discipled Apollos the way Paul had discipled them. They were the ideal people to help Apollos, though they might have felt a bit intimidated by his intellect. And being instructed in the Scriptures by a lay couple, especially a woman, could have been an uncomfortable experience for the scholarly Apollos. Priscilla must have been extraordinarily tactful, and they must have both been skillful in balancing praise and correction.

7. Obviously their joint mentoring of Apollos was successful, because what did Apollos do after this short remedial theology course? (See Acts 18:27–28.)

he greatly was then able to help those in Achaia

What an example Priscilla is of stewardship not only of her home, but of her knowledge of truth. In a private setting in partnership with her husband, the Lord gave her the privilege of helping to prepare a man for his public ministry. I know a modern Priscilla who travels with her husband training local congregations to reach their communities with the gospel. She serves mostly in a support role, but her passion for their calling is equal to her husband's, and they make a great team. They work side-by-side serving Christ, and He is giving them multiplied fruit in the lives of others.

Apollos became such an effective traveling preacher and ardent defender of the faith that some began to think of him as a competitor of Paul, Peter, and even of Christ. (See 1 Corinthians 1:12 and 3:4.) But Paul called Apollos his coworker.

> Who then is Paul, and who is Apollos, but ministers by whom ye believed, even as the Lord gave to every man? I have planted, Apollos watered; but God gave the increase. (1 Corinthians 3:5–6)

I've heard men in ministry give tribute to the influence and guidance of older folks in their early preaching days, and those helpers include godly women. While he was studying for the ministry, my husband Dave was riding his bike to a summer school class on a hot Memphis morning when he stopped to help an older lady struggling with fallen branches in her yard. He and Mrs. Laura Thompson quickly discovered that they both loved the Lord, and that summer morning a special friendship began. This loving widow gave him books, timely encouragement, and her constant prayers while he prepared to serve the Lord.

After we married and moved to Wisconsin to plant a church, she began praying for both of us. While we were on a trip home to Memphis, we visited dear Mrs. Thompson. As we sat talking on her sun porch, she told us we should never worry about a thing because, "Every morning I wake up early, have a drink of water, then lie back down on my bed, look up to the Lord, and talk to Him about little David and little Claudia way up there in wicked old Milwaukee!" We knew she loved us, knew God heard her prayers, and we were encouraged.

Is there a young man studying to serve Christ, or couple in their first ministry, who could use your encouragement and counsel, your prayers (and maybe even a bit of money) right now?

To Think and Talk About

Priscilla had a husband, but that isn't a prerequisite to serving the Lord. What are the advantages of singleness for church ministry? (See 1 Corinthians 7:32–35 and 1 Timothy 5:5, 10.) What women do you know who are good examples of this?

Aquila and Priscilla started more than another business in Ephesus. While there with Priscilla and Aquila, Paul wrote a letter back to the church at Corinth where they had previously lived and worked. At the end of the letter Paul passed along hearty greetings from this couple and also from another group.

8. Who was that? (See 1 Corinthians 16:19.)

a church gathering in their house

They weren't yet through moving around to help churches. Paul's epistle to the church at Rome ends with greetings to folks he knew there, and Priscilla and Aquila are near the top of that long list in Romans 16:3–5.

8. What does he call them?

Fellow workers

What had they done for him?

risked their lives for him

We don't know the details about that incident, but others must have known all about it, because who else appreciated them?

the churches of the Gentiles.

What were they doing in Rome (again)?

starting a church in their home.

Apparently the Lord had still one more move for them to make. We find out about it in Paul's final epistle to Timothy, who was then pastoring in Ephesus. It had been about sixteen years since Paul had first met Aquila and Priscilla at Corinth, and he was now in a Roman prison awaiting execution by Nero. In the final paragraph of his final letter, one of his final greetings (2 Timothy 4:19) was to—you guessed it! They were once again living in Ephesus.

Paul's relationship to Timothy was special. Earlier, Paul had discipled him as they traveled together on missionary journeys. His two letters to Timothy show the love of a father for his "own son in the faith" (1 Timothy 1:2) and his careful, compassionate instruction of this young pastor. 2 Timothy reveals that Paul may have been concerned about some spiritual weakness he saw in Timothy, for he encouraged him to hold fast to the doctrine he knew (1:13), to stand strong and endure suffering (2: 1, 3), to preach fearlessly (4:2), and to complete all he'd been called to do (4:5). And there in the congregation to help this young man finish strong were Aquila and Priscilla.

Every pastor I know would be thrilled to have Aquila and Priscilla in his church. They were two of those salt-of-the-earth folks that form the backbone of every strong church. They were not public speakers. In fact, we have no record of any words they spoke. But they spent their lives working side by side, investing themselves in the lives of others. Priscilla was as essential as her husband in their ministry of helps. Her obedience to God's guidelines for women in the church certainly did not stifle her usefulness. May we be as faithful as Priscilla in knowing, sharing, and living God's Word.

Epilogue

Take a bow! Give yourself a hand! You have completed this study of woman's role on God's stage, from the Garden of Eden to the Gospels to the church. I hope that you have arrived at this point with two heartfelt desires:

- To fulfill the role God has given you as a woman with contentment and passion, knowing that you are loved and cherished by your Creator, valued and adored beyond words, and exquisitely designed to bring Him glory by serving Him in the place He has prepared for you.
- To continue to study God's Word so you can learn even more about His will for you as a woman. There's life-changing truth hiding in its pages, rich treasure waiting to be discovered.

> More to be desired are they than gold, yea, than much fine gold: sweeter also than honey and the honeycomb. (Psalm 19:10)

Dig out His principles and live by them. They are His script for you, written so you will know how to obey and honor Him as you play the role of a godly woman—the role of a lifetime.

Appendix

SELECTED USES OF ‘EZER IN SCRIPTURE

The Hebrew word *’ezer* means *help.* (indicated in **bold**). Notice that the first time the word is used in Scripture, it refers to a wife, Eve. In every other use, it refers to God Himself.

Genesis 2:18
And the Lord God said, It is not good that the man should be alone; I will make him an **help** meet for him.

Genesis 2:20
And Adam gave names to all cattle, and to the fowl of the air, and to every beast of the field; but for Adam there was not found an **help** meet for him.

Exodus 18:4
And the name of the other was Eliezer; for the God of my father, said he, was mine **help**, and delivered me from the sword of Pharaoh.

Deuteronomy 33:7
And this is the blessing of Judah: and he said, Hear, Lord, the voice of Judah, and bring him unto his people: let his hands be sufficient for him; and be thou an **help** to him from his enemies.

Deuteronomy 33:26
There is none like unto the God of Jeshurun, who rideth upon the heaven in thy **help**, and in his excellency on the sky.

Psalm 33:20
Our soul waiteth for the Lord: he is our **help** and our shield.

Psalm 70:5
But I am poor and needy: make haste unto me, O God: thou art my **help** and my deliverer; O Lord, make no tarrying.

Psalm 115:9–11
O Israel, trust thou in the Lord: he is their **help** and their shield. O house of Aaron, trust in the Lord: he is their **help** and their shield. Ye that fear the Lord, trust in the Lord: he is their **help** and their shield.

Psalm 121:1–2
I will lift up mine eyes unto the hills, from whence cometh my **help**. My **help** cometh from the Lord, which made heaven and earth.

Psalm 124:8
Our **help** is in the name of the Lord, who made heaven and earth.

Psalm 146:5
Happy is he that hath the God of Jacob for his **help**, whose hope is in the Lord his God.

Compiled by Cindy Garland

Endnotes

Chapter 2

1. Adam Clarke, *Adam Clarke's Commentary* (Grand Rapids: Baker Publishing, 1967), Power Bible Software, note on Matthew 19:4.
2. Jani Ortlund, *Fearlessly Feminine* (Colorado Springs: Multnomah Books, 2000), 83.
3. Rebecca Jones, *Does Christianity Squash Women?* (Nashville: Broadman & Holman Publishers, 2005), 40.

Chapter 3

1. Henry C. Thiessen, *Lectures in Systematic Theology,* revised by Vernon D. Doerksen (Grand Rapids: Eerdmans, 1979), 176.

Chapter 4

1. Matthew Henry, *Matthew Henry's Concise Commentary on the Whole Bible* (Nashville: Thomas Nelson Publishers, 1997), 6.
2. Robert Jamieson, A. R. Fausett, and David Brown, *Jameison-Fausset-Brown Commentary* (Peabody, MA: Hendrickson Publishers, 1997), Power Bible Software, note on Genesis 3:13.
3. *New England Primer* (Boston: Massachusetts Sabbath School Society, 1784), 7.
4. C. H. Spurgeon, *Morning and Evening: Daily Readings* (Blacksburg, VA: Wilder Publications, 2008), 196–97.

Chapter 5

1. John Piper and Wayne Grudem, *Recovering Biblical Manhood and Womanhood* (Wheaton: Crossway Books, 1991), 47.
2. Henry M. Morris, *The Genesis Record* (San Diego: Creation-Life, 1976), 119.

3. Jones, 42.
4. Alexander Rattray Hay, *The Woman's Ministry in Church and Home* (Audubon, NJ: New Testament Missionary Union, 1962), 31.
5. *The Book of Common Prayer* (New York: Oxford University Press, 1928), 300.

. . . AND A CHANGE OF SCENERY

1. Dwight M. Pratt, "Women," *International Standard Bible Encyclopedia* (Grand Rapids: Eerdmans, 1979), Power Bible Software.
2. Jones, 98.

CHAPTER 6

1. Ben Witherington, *Women in the Ministry of Jesus (*Cambridge: Cambridge University Press, 1984), 10.
2. Werner Forster, *Palestinian Judaism in New Testament Times*, trans. Gordon E. Harris (London: Oliver and Boyd, 1964), 124.
3. Oswald Chambers, *My Utmost for His Highest* (Uhrichsville, OH: Barbour Publishing, 2000), devotional for November 6.
4. Henry W. Frost, *Miraculous Healing: Why does God Heal Some and Not Others?* (Grand Rapids: Revell, 1939), 37–39.
5. Hay, 38.

CHAPTER 7

1. A. T. Robertson, *Robertson's Word Pictures* (Nashville: Holman Reference, 1958), Power Bible Software, note on Mark 5:24.
2. Joseph M. Scriven, "What a Friend We Have in Jesus" (1855).

CHAPTER 8

1. *Family Bible Notes* (public domain), Power Bible Software, note on Luke 7:12.
2. Robertson, note on John 4:27.

ANOTHER INTERMISSION

1. Charles Caldwell Ryrie, *The Role of Women in the Church* (Chicago: Moody Press, 1978), 32.

CHAPTER 9

1. H. L. Willimington, *Willmington's Guide to the Bible* (Carol Stream, IL: Tyndale House, 1984), 706.
2. Ryrie, 32.